"I deeply understand what it feels like when hard stretches of life come in like a flood and cover everything with uncertainty and painful disappointment. My dear friend Nicki understands this too, and that's why she's the right person to lead us with wisdom from His Word when we feel like we are drowning in doubt and getting dangerously close to walking away from faith. This is the book your heart needs right now. I truly love this message."

Lysa TerKeurst, #1 *New York Times* bestselling author
and president of Proverbs 31 Ministries

"After reading *Flooded*, I placed this book at the edge of the bookshelf because I knew I would need its vulnerable wisdom again and again. Nicki takes a familiar story of obedience, in and out of the storm, and walks us through her own downpour. She has given us a map for navigating the roads when the rains begin to fall and do not seem to let up. *Flooded* reminds us chapter after chapter that God is with us and He is faithful."

Jamie B. Golden, cohost of *The Popcast* and *The Bible Binge*

"We know what it feels like when life gets hard. Sometimes it gets there and it stays there. And yet, difficult days don't have to define who you are when you are prepared for them. That's what Nicki does here in the pages of *Flooded*. She gives you actual, practical steps to be ready for the seasons you didn't see coming. There's no easy way to tackle tough times, but if you'll invest the time it takes to read *Flooded*, you won't have to freak out when you're facing a trial because this book will help prepare your mind and your heart for all that life throws at you."

Clayton and Sharie King, authors, speakers,
missionaries, pastors, parents

"For the brokenhearted woman who is weary from the nonstop waves of difficulty in her life, Nicki Koziarz has provided a practical roadmap for holding on to hope. In *Flooded*, Nicki will help you deal with doubt, build up your belief, and restore your soul with reminders that expectation and confidence in Christ are still possible during hard times. If you are in the middle of a storm, Nicki's personal stories along with the truth of God's Word will give you peace and remind you that even during seasons of rough water, God always offers a rainbow after the rain."

Chrystal Evans Hurst, bestselling author and speaker

"Reading this book was like sitting around the table with an old friend. We laughed, cried, and shared like only friends do. Then, after I had been poured into, I left the table with a heart full of hope. It's a powerful, life-changing read for anyone who has ever struggled to believe when life is hard."

Susan Davidson, *Flooded* focus group participant

"This book is a must read! Nicki beautifully takes us on a journey that compels us to look at ourselves, our circumstances, and the God of the impossible, all through the eyes of Noah. I recommend this book because there isn't another one on the market that captures the insight, perspective, and *just plain honesty* of saying yes to the impossible."

Demetria Stallings, worship leader,
speaker, and purpose coach

"I remember when Nicki first started brainstorming this project that had the biblical account of Noah at the center. I'll be honest, I thought, *Is there really anything more that can be learned from Noah?!* What happened over the next few hours was life changing for me as Nicki presented an aspect of Noah I never considered. What Nicki has written throughout the pages of

Flooded is not just brilliant theology, but theology that meets the heart of humanity in a profound way. This is theology at its very best! As you read *Flooded* you will find yourself on a walk with God and be met with an assuring reminder of God's mercy and grace at the turn of each page."

Joel Muddamalle, director of theological research, Proverbs 31 Ministries

"Through the account of Noah, Nicki challenges us to recognize how doubt and unbelief can creep into our souls. She then invites us into the process of change. If you have been held hostage by disbelief, doubt, or unbelief, or even wondered *Why God?*, this book will leave you hearing how God speaks hope into our circumstances, giving us something and Someone to hold on to."

Sharee Gaiser, *Flooded* focus group participant, Australia

Flooded

Other Helpful, Inspiring Books from Nicki Koziarz

5 Habits of a Woman Who Doesn't Quit

A Woman Who Doesn't Quit Bible Study

*Why Her? 6 Truths We Need to Hear When Measuring Up
Leaves Us Falling Behind*

*Rachel & Leah Bible Study: What Two Sisters Teach Us
about Combating Comparison*

*Flooded Study Guide: The 5 Best Decisions to Make
When Life Is Hard and Doubt Is Rising*

Flooded

THE 5 BEST DECISIONS
TO MAKE WHEN LIFE IS
HARD AND DOUBT IS RISING

Nicki Koziarz

BETHANYHOUSE
a division of Baker Publishing Group
Minneapolis, Minnesota

© 2021 by Nicki Koziarz

Published by Bethany House Publishers
11400 Hampshire Avenue South
Bloomington, Minnesota 55438
www.bethanyhouse.com

Bethany House Publishers is a division of
Baker Publishing Group, Grand Rapids, Michigan

Printed in the United States of America

Library of Congress Cataloging-in-Publication Data
Names: Koziarz, Nicki, author.
Title: Flooded : the 5 best decisions to make when life is hard and doubt is rising / Nicki Koziarz.
Description: Minneapolis, Minnesota : Bethany House, a division of Baker Publishing Group, [2021]
Identifiers: LCCN 2020046868 | ISBN 9780764236471 (trade paperback) | ISBN 9780764238567 (casebound) | ISBN 9781493430161 (ebook)
Subjects: LCSH: Trust—Religious aspects—Christianity. | Decision making—Religious aspects—Christianity. | Attitude (Psychology)
Classification: LCC BF575.T7 K69 2021 | DDC 158.2—dc23
LC record available at https://lccn.loc.gov/2020046868

Cover design by Kara Klotz and Alison Fargason

The author is represented by the Brock, Inc. Agency.

21 22 23 24 25 26 27   7 6 5 4 3 2 1

In keeping with biblical principles of creation stewardship, Baker Publishing Group advocates the responsible use of our natural resources. As a member of the Green Press Initiative, our company uses recycled paper when possible. The text paper of this book is composed in part of post-consumer waste.

To my husband, Kris.
May we never stop believing God for the impossible.

Some Thank-Yous

Kris, thank you for helping me sort through the "committee" in my head while I wrote this book. You have no idea how much I've come to understand the last few years how well you balance me out. And to my girls, Taylor, Hope, and Kennedy. You are my greatest joy in life. Thank you for being kind to your momma through this book-writing process.

Meredith Brock, thank you for believing in me. Thank you for walking with me on this hard road to these pages in this book. Your support and your confidence in me make me feel like everything will be okay. I appreciate your wisdom, understanding, and brilliance on all.the.things.

Lysa TerKeurst, thank you for your wisdom and for pouring into of my life. This is something I never take for granted. Thank you for helping me be a better writer, and thank you for believing in me and this message.

David Abernathy, thank you for making sure this is all theologically sound. I've learned so much from you through this process, and I don't take your input lightly. You have corrected me in the kindest ways when I've been wrong about a verse and helped me see things through a lens beyond my own understanding.

Krista, thank you for sitting with me on deck three and helping me find the gold in the text.

To my focus group, this book is better because of you. Thank you for your honesty, input, and encouragement.

Kristi D., Elle, Holly, and Kayley, thank you for being willing to always say yes to revival. May our generation never be the same because of our obedience as a team.

Jeff and Bethany team, thank you for being the kindest publishing team. I'm thankful for this opportunity to partner together.

Rebecca I., you saved the day. You are wise beyond your years and this book is better because of you.

Contents

Contents

A Letter to Flooded Readers

Hi.

Welcome to Flooded. *The book that almost drowned me.*

The night before I turned this book in to my publisher, I cried myself to sleep for the first time in years. Not because I was sad, grieved, or upset about this book. But because this has been the hardest thing I've ever done professionally. I wrote these words through the suicide of my brother, a worldwide pandemic, a national race crisis, plus a dozen other hard, personal things.

My head has felt anything but clear through this process. The craziest distractions met me every time I sat down at this keyboard to type, and doubt has lingered again and again. The Scriptures I unpack in this book were above my head, and I've never had to study something so hard to make sense of it.

This book is some of the most hard but holy work I've ever done.

I've written other books, but I want you to know a book on Noah was actually the first book idea I ever had.

I pitched a book on Noah about six years ago and got a resounding no from publishers. I didn't understand why . . . until now. In the book of Esther, one verse has turned into an anthem for seasons: For such a time as this *(Esther 4:14). This message has felt a little too timely for this moment and beyond. And a little too raw for the places in life I've walked through while writing it. So no matter how much I wanted this concept published six years ago, I know now, this is the time. Because the timing of God is never rushed by the impatience of man.*

I don't know what your life is looking like the day you begin holding this book in your hands, but I'm confident a few hard, impossible things are stirring doubt within you, because doubt isn't a seasonal struggle and doesn't come or go based on the temperature of our culture.

Doubt can only be removed by making the decision to do so.

And that is what we'll do through this book. We'll study closely the life of Noah and, based on his actions, unpack five decisions he made. These decisions are simple but hard. As the tears hit my pillowcase the night before turning this in, I had to remind myself to make these decisions, or else doubts about this whole process would indeed drown me.

I use these decisions daily. I have them written on a sticky note next to my computer, and they've helped me sort through these hard days with hope. On the other side of this book, you will be stronger, wiser, and able to deflect the detrimental things doubt can do to your soul.

I've divided this book into five sections. There are three chapters in each section. Take this one section at a time, because each section unpacks one of the five decisions. There are places for you to reflect and think throughout the book, but if you want to take the application and study process deeper, I highly recommend grabbing the accompanying study guide and video series for this book.

I have a lot of hopes for you as the reader of this message, but my greatest hope is that God would meet you on these pages and change something deep in you that doubt has tried to destroy.

You all in?

Well, then, let's get going. . . .

Nicki

To Walk with God

CHAPTER 1

The Mess of You

What if I told you, it's *you*?

You are actually the greatest struggle you will ever have to overcome in your life.

Way to ease into this, right? I mean, usually these types of conversations have a more comfortable and slow beginning. But sometimes we just need someone to be honest and upfront with us about where we're at in our process and then get going with the plan to allow change to begin. I learned this the hard way, and I wish someone had sat me down and said these things I'm about to share.

There are days when it will feel as though life has been exceptionally unkind to you. If those hard days extend into a long season, life will try to convince you it has a new rhythm. One that makes you feel offbeat every step you take. Life can often feel like a bully, throwing punches at us we didn't see coming. We get taken out, for a moment. But how we jump back in becomes our decision.

A few months ago, I was dancing to that very offbeat, unkind rhythm of life, but I thought I was hiding it well. I cried in private but praised in public. I smiled when I didn't want to. But I pulled away from the people who knew me best because I knew they would see it.

You know what it's like when an ache inside you won't leave, and it gets harder and harder to hide it? We buy the best beauty products our wallets allow, and we try to wear clothes to make us feel put together. But our lack-of-sleep-induced-bags under our eyes show we're not dancing through life like we thought we were.

It's those seasons when we post the yellow sticky notes on our mirror that say: FIND JOY TODAY. All in hopes that even though we are living in the valley of hard things, consumed with doubt, somehow we can hide it if we just put our mind in the right direction.

But living in doubt about your own faith and belief can change a person's countenance. So we fake it until we make it through. Because none of us want to be "that person," right? The person who always has an issue about something.

I thought I had people fooled.

Until.

I clicked "post" on a picture.

It was a picture of me with happy news. News I couldn't wait to share with my friends. I looked at the picture carefully before I posted it. Put just the right amount of a filter on it. It still looked like "me," but the filter provided a much better version of me, with smooth skin and color enhancement. You know, a girl's gotta do what a girl's gotta do with her camera filters.

Within seconds of my posting the picture, a message popped into my direct messages. And it was a very unexpected response.

I knew the sender personally, and honestly expected her message to say, "So happy for you!" Or something cheerleader-ish like that. But her words stung.

"I can see it in your eyes, you're not okay. This isn't the Nicki we all love."

22

I was trying to share happy news, and that was her response? Frustrated, I deleted her message and "muted" all of her posts so I wouldn't have to think about her for a long time. (Gosh, doesn't social media make us act like we're in sixth grade again? Super mature, Nicki.) But months later, as I looked back at the picture, I realized she wasn't wrong. You *could* see it in my eyes. There was a sadness no filter could hide.

I know you've had those seasons when it just feels like hard things pile on top of each other. You are afraid to open your phone because every time you do, it's another head-spinning situation to sort through. It was one of those.

In a two-year span, my mom had a six-month terminal battle with a brain tumor, my last living grandparent passed away, and my only brother tried to commit suicide four times. He lost his battle with mental illness and addiction soon after I began writing these words in this book.

There were a dozen other hard things to sort through, and it was hard day after hard day. They say your eyes are the window to your soul. My eyes were flooded with unbelief from a well of doubt deep in my soul.

Life felt like it was a daily gift of unwrapping disappointments. Isolation met me every morning. And the title of *Christian* felt very off-brand for me. Surely God saw how weary I was, right? Why wasn't He doing anything about it?

Doubt had packed all my bags and taken me on the trip of a lifetime. Except it wasn't a vacation on an exotic island—more like a TV show: *Vacation Nightmares*. I began to wonder if God really did care about all this hard stuff.

We all have to fight through hard days. But have your hard days left the lingering effect of doubt in your eyes?

At the end of hard days, it is still you versus you.

Sometimes we're the mess. And sometimes we have to be the mop. No one will clean up these messy-soul places for us.

23

> Godly strength comes from deciding to rise above the hard and pursue the holy.

The strongest people in my life are the ones who know how to win battles behind closed doors that no one knows about. They know how to rise above the hard and pursue the holy. And they know bad days do not equal a bad life.

You and I are about to become one of these people, because each of these five decisions in this book will lead us toward this goal. But just like with any goal, there will be challenges.

The Gift in Hard Days

Hard days can become the intersection of where *what was* and *what is* meets. The past often knocks on the door of the present to remind us of something we have forgotten about ourselves. Growth isn't always something new. It can be remembering what was covered up by the destruction of doubt.

A few weeks after I posted the picture and my friend made her comment, someone sent me a few pictures from my childhood. The past gently knocked on my door as I opened the package of pictures. Life looked pretty simple in those pictures, such a vast difference from the complicated life I'd find myself in thirty-five years later.

For a few moments, I was held hostage by one image. It was the little version of Nicki, with an undeniable presence of belief in that little girl's eyes. She was bossy too. Hands on her hips, a sassy smile, and eyes sending a wordless message: *Nothing is going to stop me.*

As I looked at the picture, I had to ask myself the hard question, Where is that belief-filled girl?

When was the last time you looked at a picture of yourself and saw the real you? Maybe you didn't even see the belief is gone.

You're waking up every day, going through the motions. Nothing is tragically wrong *today*, but you don't feel like yourself.

It feels like something's missing, and you can't quite put your finger on what's wrong. You find yourself looking in the mirror at a reflection that makes you feel lost.

> Just because we don't like God's ways doesn't mean we can't trust His ways.

Because maybe God has done some stuff we just don't like but we don't feel brave enough to admit it.

It's easy to trust God when our prayers are answered and life seems like a neatly folded pile of laundry. But when we don't like His ways, it's hard to trust His ways.

The good news is, Jesus has always been in the business of helping the lost become found. It's a gift to know He's here to find us in our mess and that He will help us clean up this messy-soul place.

Maybe your belief is just fine; I hope so. But if you're nodding your head yes to any of this . . . let's keep going.

Challenged to Change

If we're just meeting for the first time in these pages, besides being a woman who wrestles with doubt, I'm a wife and a mom. My husband, Kris, and I own a small farm just outside of Charlotte, North Carolina, that we call the Fixer Upper Farm.

We are first-generation farmers, which is a fancy way to say we have no clue what we're doing. But it's fun figuring it out. Our family is also in the process of adoption. I hope one day I'll be able to share more about it with you.

I also speak at churches and conferences.

One of my favorite places I've ever gotten to do this was in Haiti. And it came in the midst of that two-year battle of what felt like impossible, hard situations.

During one of the worship services, my doubt was challenged to change. If you've never heard Haitians worship before, it is truly one of the holiest things my ears have ever experienced.

While standing in this service worshiping with them before I was going to speak, my faith felt fake. I knew my mountain of doubt needed to come down.

One of the pastors shared this verse:

"Because of your little faith," he told them. "For truly I tell you, if you have faith the size of a mustard seed, you will tell this mountain, 'Move from here to there,' and it will move. Nothing will be impossible for you."

Matthew 17:20 CSB

Mustard-seed faith sounds so small. Doable. Easy. Right? And I thought I had it. But I couldn't seem to move any of the impossible mountains in my life. I have no official answers to offer you as to why.

Except, I held this Bible verse out of context and, honestly, not from a pure heart. Sometimes we just want to say to all our doubt, NOTHING IS IMPOSSIBLE FOR GOD. And then snap our fingers and watch life become all we dreamed it could be. But that's not how this verse works.

If we were to read all of Matthew 17, we would see Jesus was speaking to His disciples after they were discouraged with doubt because they couldn't heal a little boy. Jesus explains that their doubt blocked their ability to display God's power.

It's important to be curious enough to wonder why Jesus would use the example of the mustard seed to explain faith to His disciples. Side note: If you're not familiar with who the disciples were, to put it into modern terms, they were Jesus' people. Twelve guys He was equipping and training to carry on His mission once He left this earth.

Jesus wasn't saying His disciples could move an actual mountain. He was speaking metaphorically and in terms they would understand. But isn't it neat that, even today, we refer to the big, hard things in life as mountains?

Jesus is still speaking our language.

The thing that's so fascinating about the mustard seed is what it can turn into and how fast it can grow.

> Mustard-seed faith isn't a quantity of faith; it's a quality of faith.

According to the gardening website hunker.com, mustard seeds can sprout within three to ten days. They grow very rapidly, and the leaves can be eaten in salads. The longer they grow, the bigger they grow, up to forty-five inches high.[1]

Jesus is telling His disciples it's not about the size of their faith. He's not necessarily looking for BIG FAITH, BIG DREAMS kinda people. He partners with people who have this little tiny spark of faith and, if planted right, can become something way beyond who they are. The ones who are willing to look at hard situations and say, "With God, it's possible." It's a quality of faith, not a quantity.

That day in Haiti, I sensed God was asking me to repent from fake faith. It was my challenge to change.

God's kindness in the midst of so much hard is often found in the most unusual ways.

Repentance is one of those places we can miss God's kindness. I've resisted that word, *repent*, for so long because my religious roots had some background where that word was very misused. But I found out one of the definitions of the word *repent* is "to change one's mind."

Unknowingly, based on my circumstances, I had changed my mind about some things about God. I had partnered with fear, anxiety, and doubt—things that make it hard to believe in God's power.

And it would be my decision in that moment to re-change my mind. To remember God is who He says He is, despite what my circumstances say.

That is God's kindness in this process. To allow us to experience changing our mind, again and again. God offers us this same kindness today.

What is something you might need to re-change your mind about God? _____

Change What You Choose

Repentance stops us from being a prisoner to doubt. It shouldn't shame us, guilt-trip us, or make us feel worse about ourselves. Like that day in Haiti for me, in a moment, in a single day, everything can change for us because we seek repentance and gain a changed-by-God mind.

Once we know better, we should do better, right? But what we aren't changing, we are choosing. I'm desperate for change and I know you are too.

There's possibly another factor playing into this challenged-to-change struggle for you: isolation. I've wondered about those places where you push yourself into isolation because you can't bear the thought of letting someone into this place with you.

You're tired of Prayer Requester Patsy asking you what she can pray for, and you just keep looking at all your problems, thinking you shouldn't bother. *It's too messy. Too complicated. Besides, other people are dealing with more "serious" issues. I'm not worth the fuss of a prayer request.*

I get you. And I'm with you. But will you let others into this process with you too? Sometimes the hardest step we can take to change our minds is to ask others to help us get there.

People don't want to listen to complaining, but they are eager to listen to change. Stay close to people who love you enough to challenge you to change.

I have some solutions to offer you, not based on my experience, but on someone else's. Seeing this doubt-struggle clearly in my life, I did what this unlikely Bible

> Stay close to people who love you enough to challenge you to change.

teacher does best. I went to the Bible and found someone with a more impossible situation to overcome than we have.

I think sometimes we are looking for mentors, counselors, and pastors to help us (which isn't always bad), but we forget the countless people of faith in the Scriptures who have gone before us with the same struggles.

Before there was a Bible, there were people who demonstrated faith that changed the world through their belief based on what they didn't even know.

Today, we have a Bible in a world demonstrating faith by sitting with theology that settles our belief based on what we do know.

And it's not working.

About a thousand years ago, St. Anselm said, "I do not seek to understand in order that I may believe, but rather, I believe in order that I may understand." Not much has changed in the human heart searching for resolve with this struggle to understand.

I think we need to look back at a man who can teach us a few things about belief.

Noah.

Because of his obedience to God, humanity was saved.

In most of the Scriptures we'll study, we don't actually have a lot of words from Noah. We can see his actions, though.

And actions stem from decisions. So, based on his actions—his obedience to God—we'll unpack five decisions we can make when life is hard and doubt is rising.

I'm not sure God is asking any of us, like He did Noah, to save humanity (thank goodness), but there's something hard He's asking us to believe Him through. And doubt will attempt to rise every step you take.

The problem is still going to be . . . you.

Will you let your belief-struggle come to the surface? Or will you keep stuffing it down like I did and mask yourself every opportunity you can get?

No beauty product, spa, or magic pill can put the spark of belief back in your eyes. Only Jesus can do that. And I know He wants to.

It's not too late. For any of us.

Where There Is Doubt

Some may want to say believing in yourself has nothing to do with believing in God. I say, wrong.

How we view ourselves is so intertwined with how we view God that we cannot separate the two. If one is off focus, they both are. Chances are, there are a few things in your soul that look a little blurry.

Hard seasons can cause us to look at God in an unhealthy way. Instead of asking God what He needs us to see in these seasons, we may constantly find ourselves asking Him if He really knows what He is doing. It's not our questions for God that lead to soul-unhealthiness, but rather our questioning of God.

My questioning often makes me wonder, *If God doesn't know what He is doing, how am I supposed to know what I am doing?*

This is what doubt will do to a person's soul.

Completely misconstrue it until it looks nothing like a soul that is confidently loved by God. And the valley of hard things will start to convince you that this is where life is to be lived. Get used to it.

But just because we are flooded with doubt doesn't mean we have to be destroyed by doubt. Where there is doubt, there is still hope, which is the way to rise.

> It's not our questions for God that lead to soul-unhealthiness, but rather our questioning of God.

God never promised us a life that was easy or simple. He promised to give us everything we would ever need to silence our doubts.

If you look at life and all you see is pain and sorrow, I think you're dealing with a heart wrestling with doubt. If you've settled for mediocre, comfortable, and expected, I think you're dealing with a heart wrestling with doubt. If God's told you to do something and it doesn't feel possible, I think you're dealing with a heart wrestling with doubt.

If you've tried all the pick-me-ups and self-help lists and motivational videos and nothing is working, it's time to try something different.

I had to figure out how to get that belief-filled girl back. And I did. I mean, she's still working on coming back, but she's a lot more here than she's not.

Your faith is still a mountain-moving faith. Doubt just made those mountains rise really fast. It's time to bring them down.

CHAPTER 2

Disbelief to Unbelief

U ntil a few months ago, I'm not sure I could say I fully understood the difference between disbelief and unbelief. I also wasn't clear what either of those things had to do with doubt. But I've come to understand the conflict in our souls that never ends is the one between belief and unbelief.

Doubt is the dangerous place we linger in the middle of the battle between the two.

If we don't understand why we have to change our mind (repent) and make intentional decisions to deflect doubt, life will continue to feel hard and impossible. Those mountains will keep rising. And we'll keep looking at them in defeat.

Let's look at the definitions of these two words and find the connection to doubt. According to dictionary.com, here are the definitions of *disbelief* and *unbelief*:

Disbelief: the inability or refusal to believe or to accept something as true.

Unbelief: the state or quality of not believing; skepticism, especially in matters of doctrine or religious faith.

Disbelief seeks you out all day long with hard-to-believe news, stories, facts, and updates. And disbelief is always in our minds, tempting us to question both ourself and God as we look at the shocking world in front of us.

We know God offers us a mustard-seed quality of faith; we just don't know if it's possible for us. This is where doubt enters. Disbelief often brings doubt in our souls, which, if not dealt with, can lead to unbelief.

Disbelief → Doubt → Unbelief

Unbelief is what causes us to turn our souls away from God. It's the most dangerous place disbelief and doubt can lead to.

The "Why Bother" Mindset

I hope you like dogs, because we need to use mine as an example to understand all this. If God can use a donkey in the Bible (Numbers 22:22–31), He can use a pug in this book. Stick with me.

Herman, our pug, is a fluffy little fawn-colored guy. His wrinkles are just enough to make him look like a loaf of bread when he's lying down. He sits on the couch like a human, and to add to his human characteristics, he has recently started walking around the house with his dog bone in his mouth as if it's a cigar. *Have mercy.*

Herman can be kinda demanding, and it's our fault.

When Herman was a puppy, the vet let us know there were several ways we could feed him, the easiest option being to just let him eat when he's hungry. Keep food in the bowl and be done with a schedule. Works great.

But because of this system, occasionally someone (ahem, mostly yours truly) forgets to put Herman's food in his bowl.

And this makes him so annoyed.

Herman, in disbelief that there is no food in his bowl, will stand at his empty bowl and hit it with his paw until one of us comes to fill it up.

Herman doesn't struggle to believe we will put food in his bowl. Herman struggles with disbelief. He just cannot believe we don't remember to put the food in the bowl every single day. Still he shows up, wondering, *What kind of humans are they?*

The way you and I show up before God reveals where we are in this disbelief-to-unbelief process.

God doesn't get annoyed with our disbelief. But are we still showing up? Or have we stopped asking and seeking because we just can't believe God hasn't answered us?

Have we taken on a *why bother* mentality?

It's this place where we trusted God with our needs, desires, wants, or miracles. And we showed up every day believing God would do what we knew He could do. But for whatever the reason, God didn't do what we had hoped. And now we've stopped praying and believing. Because, *why bother?*

I resist people who try to explain God away. Have you ever heard someone say your prayers were not answered the way you hoped because you didn't believe enough? Or have you ever listened to someone try to make sense of a tragedy? The lack of compassion I see us sometimes have for the mystery of God is something no one wants to talk about.

> Just because God hasn't answered us doesn't mean God's annoyed with us.

I get it. We want answers to our disbelief. We want justice for our prayers. We want to comfort people by helping them make sense of things that make no sense.

There are times when answers to our prayers leave us in total disbelief.

I think about the time my friend Kristi and I found ourselves next to a hospital bed of a man who was dying too young. We extended our faith and belief that God would heal him. We left his hospital room in total confidence. God was going to heal him.

And then the seed of disbelief met us that next morning when we heard he had died during the night. Honestly, because I believed so much in his healing, the next time I went to pray for someone, I had *unbelief*. Why bother to pray if God's going to do what He's going to do anyway?

And that's how it all happens. It creeps in. Step by step.

It's taken a lot of soul-searching to understand these places I've teetered on the edge of unbelief. It will for you too. But Noah's process with God helps us understand the need to recognize disbelief as it turns into doubt.

Through Noah's account, you will see that disbelief isn't necessarily wrong, but it will wreak havoc on your soul if it isn't dealt with by faith.

Second Corinthians 5:7 reminds us, faith is not about what we see in front of us because faith and sight often oppose each other.

> . . . for we walk by faith, not by sight.
>
> 2 Corinthians 5:7

Let's begin unpacking Noah's assignment and what he teaches us about our first decision: to walk with God.

Decision One: To Walk with God

How This Went Down

Listen. I am not your theological expert girl. I don't use words like *propitiation*, *regeneration*, *exegesis*, or *infralapsarian*. (I'll wait for all my friends who need to go and Google those words. Me too, sis. Not that there is a thing wrong with people who do use those words.)

If that's you, high fives.

I love God and I study His Word, but I don't use words like that. But I know how to find people who do use those theological words like the above, and I know how to ask them questions to help us make sense of things in the Bible. And that's what I did as I studied Noah—asked people wiser than I am a lot of questions.

Sometimes we read something in the Bible and think it makes no sense and none of this could be possible. Which is exactly how I felt when I opened the pages of Genesis chapter 6 to learn about Noah.

It's a chaotic scene. People were doing all kinds of bad stuff. God was mad. And then God made a decision. He was going to just clear the table. Except it wasn't dishes. It was mass destruction.

> So the LORD said, "I will blot out man whom I have created from the face of the land, man and animals and creeping things and birds of the heavens, for I am sorry that I have made them."
>
> Genesis 6:7

There's a lot we need to see in this verse. God's anger, His disappointment with humanity, and His decision. If we were to back up just a few chapters in Genesis, we would see some of the things that happened to get humanity to this place.

Keep in mind, Genesis is the first book of the Bible, so we're only six chapters into this and the world's already a mess.

In Genesis 1, the world is perfect. In Genesis 2, God sees that Adam needs someone to make life more fulfilling—enter Eve. But in Genesis 3, sin enters the world through Adam and Eve's disobedience in eating from the forbidden tree. And then in Genesis 4, we see things get worse with Adam and Eve's children Cain and Abel. And then a bunch of time passes, and we see in Genesis 5 a lot of new generations come to be.

> Noah was
> a faithful
> person, but
> he was far
> from perfect.

We don't see a play-by-play of what was happening during all that time, but it had to be really bad for us to arrive in Genesis 6:7 and read the words that God was grieved He had made humanity.

But why did God choose Noah for such a seemingly impossible assignment?

According to the Scriptures, the only perfect human who ever lived on this earth was Jesus. Because Jesus was both God and man. So Noah was a faithful person, but he was far from perfect.

Here are five other things we know for sure about Noah.

5 Things We Know about Noah

1. Noah came from a long line of faithful-to-God men. His grandfather was Methuselah, one of the oldest men to ever live (Genesis 5:27). Noah's father was Lamech. I've wondered if Noah ever had to think back on his family's faithfulness to keep going in his own belief.

2. According to Genesis 9:20, Noah was a farmer. (Ah. ME TOO. Okay. Not really.) If I've learned anything about farmers, it's how resourceful they can be. Still, Noah was NOT an ark-builder. This was a little out of Noah's realm of experience.

3. Noah was married, but we have no idea what his wife's name was. Moses wrote the verses we will be studying on Noah, but for whatever reason, this detail is left out.

4. Noah had three sons, and yes, we know their names: Ham, Shem, and Japheth (Genesis 6:10).

5. Noah preached his face off. (Okay, not really. This is just a thing we say in the South when a preacher moves the heart of people in a big way.) Noah is revealed as

a preacher of righteousness in 2 Peter 2:5. What does that mean? It means Noah spent a lot of his time telling people about the ways of God and how important it would be to follow Him.

A few things we know, a lot we don't. Now, let's unpack this belief assignment for Noah.

Noah's Belief Assignment

And God said to Noah,

> "I have determined to make an end of all flesh, for the earth is filled with violence through them. Behold, I will destroy them with the earth. Make yourself an ark of gopher wood. Make rooms in the ark, and cover it inside and out with pitch."
>
> Genesis 6:13–14

Where was Noah when God met him with this ark assignment? We don't know.

But think of what life would be like for a farmer, husband, father, and preacher. I have a feeling Noah was just going about his business, and then in one moment, with one encounter with God, life as he knew it changed.

When was the last time your life dinged with a notification that caused you to stop and ask, Do I trust God with this?

Maybe it was a text from a friend asking for prayer, a panic-inducing headline from the news, or even an opportunity to do something totally new. All of us have had a moment when one update had the potential to change everything.

God sent the notification to Noah. And this is the part where I need more details about Noah's wife—because Kris Koziarz has come home with some big ideas before that I've hated to have to bring a dose of reality to. Sometimes he listens,

> If you will decide to keep walking, God will keep working.

sometimes he doesn't. Which is why we have a fixer-upper tractor AND a fixer-upper boat sitting in our back field that have almost been the death of my sanity. It is enough to have a fixer-upper farm; we don't need anything else to fix, and I have to frequently remind him of this.

What on earth did Noah's wife say when he came home with this assignment from God?

Was she on board right away?

Did she raise her eyebrows?

Did she ask follow-up questions?

I doubt she was just like, "Sure, babe, whatever you say!" There had to be some disbelief stirring in her as well. Ultimately, she made it onto the ark, so she never got to the point where unbelief pushed her to the point of no return.

But I think there's a huge clue about how she and Noah arrived at this place of belief just a few verses before the verses of his assignment:

> But Noah found favor in the eyes of the LORD.
>
> These are the generations of Noah. Noah was a righteous man, blameless in his generation. *Noah walked with God.*
>
> Genesis 6:8–9 (italics added)

How was Noah able to rise above the doubt this assignment could have brought him? He made a decision: to walk with God.

This was not an out-for-a-few-laps-around-the-park kinda walk. It was a place in his soul where he became settled on who God was to him through a daily decision to show up before God. There was a destination Noah had in his life, and he would reach it only by walking with God.

Right now it may not be super clear where your destination is. You might just barely be surviving, and this all feels far off for you. But if you will decide to keep walking, God will keep working.

It might feel like the enemy is following your footsteps and trying to trip you up every chance he gets. But with God, you are always one step ahead of any scheme to take you down.

CHAPTER 3

Walk the Line, Barefoot

I think my brother, Mike, was the typical big brother. We grew up disliking each other, and I often found myself on the other side of his unusual "torture" tactics. Like the time he made me drink salt-and-pepper water, or he'd tell on me to my parents about something stupid I did. Despite our sibling quarrels, I always looked up to him.

I never dreamed that into our adult years, after not hearing from him for months on end, I'd find myself Googling his name to see if he was in jail or had made the news for some type of arrest or worse. Sometimes I'd even search death records to see if he was still alive.

I don't know how exactly you find yourself doing things like this or writing words like these in a book. It seems surreal, like it shouldn't be my life. And it shouldn't. This shouldn't be anyone's story, but it is again and again.

There is a very specific time in each of our lives when we realize just how much we don't believe in ourselves.

I'm not sure when that happened in Mike. But at some point, after many wrong turns, he decided life wasn't worth living.

Despite our attempts to help Mike, pointing him in the right direction and trying to help him see his worth, he couldn't see it. I don't know exactly what was going on inside him, but I know the battle kept getting fiercer.

And so, suicide harassed him. Again and again and again. Until finally it stopped making appointments with him because it fulfilled its commitment to destroy him. Or at least that's how it felt as I stood next to his hospital bed in Seattle one cold November morning.

I watched his body shut down from a bottle of pills. Heartbeat after heartbeat.

You could feel the judgment of the nurses and doctors and anyone else who entered the room. He was an addict. This wasn't his first time in their care. And I wondered if they felt their resources were being wasted on a human who didn't seem to care.

Our family had joked Mike was like the cat with nine lives. It amazed us how much he was able to live through. And so that morning as I spoke to the doctor on the phone and he said, "Nicki, I don't even know if you'll make it in time," I didn't believe him. Mike had pulled through times like this before, and I knew he had not fulfilled his purpose here on this earth.

Sometimes people say things like "When your time is up, it's up." While I agree God is sovereign and knows all, I don't believe suicide is ever part of God's plan for someone. Ever. And this is something I don't think we talk enough about. Because while God has a plan filled with good things, the enemy has a plan too. And his plan includes killing, stealing, and destroying (John 10:10).

Mike and I had the exact same upbringing. We went to church, our dad taught Sunday school, we prayed before meals, and holidays like Christmas and Easter were always about Jesus before us.

You can grow up in the church your entire life, know God, love God, and do all the God-things. But you still have to find your own way.

The Why That's in the Way

A bad accident years ago had left Mike questioning the goodness of God. He fell off a power line pole, broke his back, and was told he would never walk again. He did walk again, and his story was filled with so much hope.

But I believe his disbelief over what happened always made him wonder, *Why, God? Why me?*

While Mike physically learned to walk again, walking with God became harder and harder. Eventually, it just all became too much. He was past the point of no return. His destructive decisions had become too much of who he was.

I believe with everything in me that Mike is in heaven today. His battle with choices and mental illness did not define his eternity.

But I'm left here in the aftermath of losing him too soon. With prayers for his life that feel unanswered. And sometimes I still can't believe he's really gone, even though I saw his heart rate monitor flatline with my own eyes.

My given name, Nichole, means victory. And since I discovered the meaning of my name, I have always tried to speak into people from the place of victory. But this time? I am coming to you from a place of defeat. Not the kind of defeat that comes from quitting. Goodness, I already wrote the book on that. This kind of defeat comes regardless of everything you did right. It messes with you because it doesn't make sense. You just can't believe it.

This kind of defeat changes you. And if we don't allow it to sit with us and just sweep it under the rug instead, it can define us.

> God can handle your disbelief. And He will help you believe again.

As grief and loss have met me the last few years in the most uninvited ways, some people tried, with the best intentions, to hold out their hand to me. But they said things like "God *did* answer your prayers, just not the way you asked Him to."

Their words only left me more doubtful and full of more disbelief. What I really needed was someone to look at me and say, "Nicki, God can handle your disbelief. And He will help you believe again."

If that's you today, looking at life, full of doubt, I say those words to you: God can handle it, and He will help you believe again.

Disbelief loves for us to become spiritual victims of our circumstances. It knows that if it can hold us hostage, the next time our faith is stretched, doubt will appear. And if doubt wins, unbelief is soon to follow. And then? It's often the point of no return.

Each of us has a *Why, God?* that needs to be dealt with. So here's where we start: We tell God our *why* that is in the way of walking with Him. This *why-wedge* between you two, it needs to be gone.

This is hard soul-work. Work that won't make the enemy happy. And you may find yourself more frustrated than faithful right now. And that's okay. Just keep turning the page and we'll get there, together.

The Walking Out of Belief

According to yourdictionary.com, the idiom "walk the line" means to "maintain an intermediate position between contrasting choices, opinions, etc." The term can be traced back all the way to the 1700s when inmates were made to walk around a thick-lined circle for their "rec time." If a prisoner was found walking off the line, he was punished.

The phrase is used today in multiple ways, including song titles and even as the title of a movie about Johnny Cash. Some people use "walk the line" to make a strong point, like *get yourself together*.

Lines show up everywhere and represent so many things. Think about how many lines you encounter in a week. Lines we wait in at the grocery store, lines to pick up our kids from school, lines that divide land.

Lines are fragile, though.

And they can easily be crossed, forgotten about, or even totally missed.

In our culture today, it's not clear what it means to walk with God. There is a thin line between the ways of this world and the ways of our God. A large portion of our world believes in God but does not consider the Bible absolute truth.

According to the Pew Research Center, most of America (90 percent) believes in some type of "higher power." So belief is there. But where we start to divide rapidly is that only 56 percent of those who believe in a higher power believe in the God of the Bible.[1]

As Pew Research dug even deeper into the research, they found 69 percent of the Baby Boomer generation believes in the God of the Bible. Sixty-four percent of Generation X believes. Fifty-four percent of older millennials believe, and 50 percent of younger millennials believe in the God of the Bible.

Since my kids are part of Generation Z, I'm very curious what future stats will say. So far, research shows an incredibly rapid decrease in belief for this generation, and honestly, as a mom, I see it. I even own my responsibility in it. This generation

> There is a thin line between the ways of the world and the ways of our God.

Belief in God by Generational Group[2]

% of adults who say they believe in God . . .

Generation	Absolutely Certain	Fairly Certain	Not Too/ Not at All Certain	Don't Know	Do Not Believe in God	Other/Don't Know If They Believe in God
Younger Millennial	50%	21%	9%	< 1%	17%	3%
Older Millennial	54%	22%	7%	1%	13%	3%
Generation X	64%	20%	5%	< 1%	9%	2%
Baby Boomer	69%	18%	4%	1%	6%	2%
Silent	71%	16%	4%	2%	6%	2%
Greatest	66%	15%	4%	5%	7%	3%

is incredibly hard to speak Truth into. The church has changed, culture has changed, family units have changed, and the changes have caught most of us off guard.

We are all constantly being flooded with messages that counteract Truth. We look more at screens than we do into eyes. Anxiety is at an all-time high. Opinions are all over the internet. Temptation to doubt God is at every corner of our lives.

The thing is, this isn't new.

When I open up the biblical account of Noah, I see a world in spiritual chaos. Sin. Darkness. Confusion. Anger. Destruction. Evil. The same things we find our world swirling in today. It's a hard reality to swallow, but not much has changed in the hearts of humans since the days of Noah.

But there was one man who found a way around the chaos of humanity by doing something you and I can do today: walk with God. If it wasn't impossible for Noah, it's not impossible for you and me. But it's going to take courage to stop looking at the world around us with a blaming finger and look within.

We can blame the internet, phones, our schools, and even our churches all we want for the way Truth has been compromised. But if we're not willing to start with ourselves, what are we doing?

Walking with God shouldn't look like it did for those prisoners in the 1700s walking the line in a prison yard. If we cross the line, there's always a way back. Maybe we just need to decide to get back on the line.

Noah teaches us to make the decision to walk with God. But I want to add something to this. To get even closer to God, may we walk *barefoot*.

Take Your Shoes Off

Shoes are good. In fact, very rarely will you ever see me walking barefoot. I just love how shoes feel on my feet. I don't want cold floors messing up my comfy vibe in the winter. Flip-flops in the summer always feel right.

I also do not really like feet.

I don't like looking at feet while at the beach. And please, oh please, for goodness' sake, DO NOT take your shoes off on an airplane. I also tend to lose my cool when my family and I are cozied up on the couch watching a movie and one of them slides their naked feet onto my side of the couch.

STOP IT.

And put some socks on.

Despite my feelings about feet, did you know there are medical professionals who have the opinion that walking barefoot outside is actually good for you? If we want to get fancy with a hipster term, it's called "earthing."

Apparently, all that stuff in the soil and grass has good minerals for your body that your feet absorb when you walk. It's suggested by these pros to walk outside, barefoot, a few minutes a day to get the earth's mineral benefits for your body.

I don't know. I'm sure there's some truth to this. I'm just not ready to start identifying with the group urbandictionary.com calls the nelipot and hit the ground running, barefoot.

But I do think there's something important to understand about this.

There's a connection we can make from Noah to another man in the Bible: Moses.

Moses was an unlikely leader in the Scriptures who, like Noah, also received what probably seemed like an impossible assignment from God. Moses got his first assignment from God while standing in front of a burning bush. God was speaking through the fire, but before Moses received any instructions, God gave him a command:

> "Do not come near; take your sandals off your feet, for the place on which you are standing is holy ground."
>
> Exodus 3:5

There are many opinions why God would say this to Moses. But basically, it was a stance of humility and honor for the presence of God.

Moses didn't argue with God. He just took off his shoes and listened to the rest of what God had to say. The wild thing is, as I've been studying the passages in the Bible about Noah, I see something so similar. Until the very ending of the account of Noah, we never actually see Noah say anything in the text.

Scripturally, it is revealed to us as a pretty simple process. God commands, Noah listens. And repeat.

Is it possible we're experiencing unbelief in our lives because we haven't been willing to take a posture of humility? Maybe you're thinking, *Well, if God spoke to me through a burning bush or told me exactly what to do like He did with Noah, this would be a lot easier to figure out.* Agreed.

The reality is, this process is hard. We don't understand it all. Maybe we've never done this work in our souls before. I mean, even Noah was tasked to do something he had never done before.

Just like the hipster medical professionals telling us the benefits of walking barefoot outside, Moses is showing us the benefit of standing "barefoot" before the Lord. It's good for us.

> Whenever we make our ways or our words higher than those of God, we have fallen into pride.

Later, Moses would also build an ark (Exodus 25:10), much different from Noah's, but with a very similar purpose: God's grace in the midst of hopeless and hard.

When I think about everything that has led me to not believing in myself and in God, a lot of it has to do with pride. Here's the problem with pride: We tend to think of it as being this macho-mega-mouthy person.

But pride can also be the quiet, standing to the side, fearful soul. Too much humility is also pride. Whenever we make our ways or our words higher than those of God, we have fallen into pride.

So we're going to have to "take off our shoes" and humbly clear the way for whatever is standing between us and the holiness of our God, and it's going to feel uncomfortable.

And this is the decision you need to make in the midst of hopeless and hard: *Will you keep walking with God?*

Getting a Grip

I'm sure I was looking up something for our farm one day on YouTube when I randomly found a fascinating video about a woman named Faith Dickey.

Faith is what's called a "slackliner." At first, it might seem like she's just a tightrope walker, but she does a much more difficult version, something called "high-lining." It's walking on a flat, braided slack line across an extreme height through mountains like the Alps. Crazy!

What's extra interesting is that Faith does these incredible walks from one peak to another on a braided flat rope barefoot. Even in extremely cold temperatures, there she is, walking barefoot across an open space.

Most people who do high-lining do it barefoot. Bare feet tend to have the greatest grip on the line.

Many people are willing to say they will walk with God. But few have a grip on what it means. Noah had to have such a tight grip on this assignment that even while the rest of the world was falling apart, he wasn't.

Same for us.

I think this is what's needed in our generation today. We need people who stand out to the rest of the world. I'm not talking about taking a high-and-mighty stance and declaring to the world, I WILL NEVER WATCH THE BACHELOR, AND I AM NOT DOING THE TIKTOK. You do you. And you hold tight to what you need to hold tight to.

But, here's the not-so-shocking news . . .

We all have our things and thoughts that make us look less like Jesus. And unbelief just seems to be the acceptable, forgotten, and unrecognized sin-struggle. But it will be what brings disobedience to our stories again and again.

Faith is faith, no matter how small.

If we get the right grip, we'll be like Faith Dickey, walking from this mountain to the next.

I truly believe if faith was possible for Noah, it's possible for us. Even if it looks like a tiny mustard seed, faith is faith, no matter how small.

Each of our assignments of faith will look different. To some, it's going to be getting a grip on Truth for the first time. For others, it's going to be getting a grip on our emotions, habits, thought patterns, or words we speak.

But for all of us, it's going to be getting a grip on the daily practice of moving across the line from one mountain to the next and strengthening our faith. This is what it means to daily make a decision to walk with God.

I want you to think back to the *why* that's in your way. As we close out this chapter and section of the book, here's a prayer for us:

God, thank you that I don't have to stay in the place of disbelief, doubt, or unbelief.

Thank you for the power, authority, wisdom, and goodness Jesus brings to all situations, including mine.

So right now, I confess unbelief has convinced me that

_____ .

I repent from this thought pattern.

And I ask that you give me mustard-seed faith over this situation. I will keep walking with you.

In Jesus' name, amen.

To Listen to God

CHAPTER 4

Listen Up

If you have ever been around teenagers for any amount of time, I don't have to explain the frustrations of hearing and listening.

I love my three teenage girls.

But there is a reason why the last five years, as they've all slid into their teen years, my eyebrows have started falling out and I have to fill them in with brow-magic tools every day. I'm sure technically it has something to do with hormonal changes, but I'd be willing to go head-to-head with a medical researcher that my own hormonal changes have come from a condition called "teen-a-don't-listen."

Many times, I have stood at the bottom of our stairs to call out to the long hallway above me for one of my teenagers to come and put something away. Sometimes I think they think what I've asked is simply a suggestion, and it's normally when I use a nice tone, like "Please, come pick up your shoes."

Silence. Nothing.

I swallow my frustration with a thought like, *I'm sure they're coming.*

A few minutes later, I call to them again. Maybe she just didn't hear me. So I say it a little louder, a little firmer.

Ten minutes later, shoes still in the middle of the floor, I am officially done with my thinking the best of them and their intentions and their lack of listening and my tone changes. "GET DOWN HERE NOW AND PICK UP THESE SHOES, OR YOUR PHONE IS G-O-N-E!"

And suddenly, like Mary Poppins just snapped her fingers, a body appears at the top of the stairs and begins stomping down. "Okay, okay, I heard you! YOU DON'T HAVE TO YELL." I exhale and bite my lip to not yell even more.

Are you kidding me? I didn't *have* to yell. And all the mommas of teens said, "Mm-hmm" (while another eyebrow hair falls out).

Each day you and I are listening to something. The hard days seem to be the days when doubt shouts its greatest lies. But what you listen to often becomes the house you live in.

God is always speaking, but I do wish sometimes He would yell. Most of the time, we are the ones who struggle to listen. And this will always be a decision—to listen to God.

We saw in the last section of this book that Noah made the decision to walk with God. But the second decision we can see from his process is that he decided he would listen to what God said.

Decision Two: To Listen to God

After God expressed his grief for humanity, God explained His plan and included very specific instructions for the ark.

> "Make yourself an ark of gopher wood. Make rooms in the ark, and cover it inside and out with pitch."
>
> Genesis 6:14

Looking back to Genesis 6:1–7, we see God gave *the way* He would save humanity. He was going to make the earth right again through a flood that would cover the entire earth—a clean slate. Whether Noah agreed with God or not wasn't the issue.

God had a way, and it would be up to Noah to listen to the way.

But I also see God giving Noah a word of hope.

I don't know if this is just a Southern thing, but have you ever heard someone trying to make a decision or walking through something hard say, "I just need a word from the Lord!"? Meaning, they needed something encouraging from God (a word) to help them believe and trust in His way.

In Genesis 6:9–22, God gave Noah a word of hope.

The word of hope was that Noah, his family, and almost seven thousand creatures would be saved. This word was the space of hope tucked into this incredibly hard way. In fact, this was the revelation of God's mercy—that He wasn't going to do away with humanity period. And because of this way and word, you and I are here on this earth today. Grace and mercy, for sure.

There was a way and there was a word.

As God speaks to you about your disbelief that has turned into doubt, He will show you a way back to belief. He will give you hope to hold on to.

But when God speaks, He often speaks a word—like He did to Noah—that requires a brave act of obedience on our part. Obeying God is the thing you'll have to convince your heart to not be afraid of. But the greatest peace comes after the hardest things are surrendered.

When Listening Doesn't Make Sense

Arks easily can be confused with a boat or ship, but an ark was different in one specific way: There is nothing to steer in an ark. Ships and boats all have steering mechanisms. An ark needs to float, stay balanced, and be able to hold a lot of cargo. Ships and boats do similar things, but they have specific destinations.

Noah's assignment was to build something that would last and sustain them during this long season. But the destination of the ark is something we never see God show Noah in the Scriptures. That's another struggle with listening to God. In the moment, the way seems to not have a clear destination. Listening becomes hard because we don't know exactly where we're going.

But remember, when God gives a way, He gives a word.

One of the most comforting things I see in Noah's process is that he didn't try to make sense of it. He rolled with it all.

> You don't have to have the spiritual superpower of making sense of the hard things to do the hard things.

Think about the massiveness of the assignment God gave Noah. Not just the physical building of the ark assignment, which we'll get to in a second, but the emotional and spiritual side too. Yet somehow Noah stopped trying to make sense of it and just stepped into it.

I find myself weary of people trying so hard to make sense of God. It is painful enough to walk through circumstances that don't make any sense, like losing someone tragically, only to have someone try to make sense of it by tagging it with a statement like "We just never know how our loss is somehow heaven's gain."

I am 100 percent **not here** for the over-spiritualizing of hopes that have not been fulfilled. Most of our hearts need a place to land that says, *I don't get this either, and I'm not going to try to make sense of God.*

You don't have to have the spiritual superpower of making sense of the hard things to do the hard things.

There will be things on this side of eternity that will never make sense to us. It doesn't mean we had it wrong or we didn't listen to God. That's the story doubt wants to tell us.

Exhale the sense-shouting as much as you need to. And listen to the whisper of faith that says, *God knows what He's doing.* Trust what you hear.

This Is Yours

We live in a world that needs to shout about everything the moment it happens. Thank you, social media, for that. But right now, your doubt-defeating assignment, like Noah's, is just between you and God. It's nobody else's business . . . yet. You are learning to listen in a way that will build your faith to be able to receive step one, then step two, and so on.

Notice that Genesis 6:14 says, "Make yourself . . ." God did not tell Noah to contract out this assignment. It was Noah's. He was to carry it out from beginning to end, and it will be the same for you. While there are times to bring in the experts, at the very beginning, in this sacred place God has you right this moment, this is just between you and Him.

God gives Noah the first step. Noah doesn't freak out, run away, or send his wife to the market to buy up everything they might need. He listens. Takes notes, I'm sure. And then God gives Noah the next few very specific steps.

> This is how you are to make it: the length of the ark 300 cubits, its breadth 50 cubits, and its height 30 cubits. Make a roof for the ark, and finish it to a cubit above, and set the door of the ark in its side. Make it with lower, second, and third decks.
>
> Genesis 6:15–16

If reading about all these cubits and heights and widths makes you break out in hives because it makes no sense (hand raised), let's just take a moment to visualize a football field and a half. That's about how long the ark was to be. The height was over fifty feet high, like a four-story office building.

I'm a visual learner, and I knew I needed a more intense visual of this. So I rallied up three of my friends, packed myself a bag, and we flew to a place in Kentucky called the Ark Encounter. If you haven't heard of the Ark Encounter, it is one of the most fascinating places I've ever been to that brings biblical history to life, specifically the account of Noah. Put the Ark Encounter on your bucket list, for sure.

The wise leaders of the Ark Encounter have taken many years to study and understand what the ark most likely looked like. They fully admit there's no way to know for sure, but I'm telling you, there's something so holy about this place.

Most of the time being an author means sitting behind a screen in the same stretchy pants you wore the day before and staring at words like *the*, wondering if you used them correctly. Writing books is nothing shiny. But occasionally, being an author has a fun perk. When my publisher let the Ark Encounter people know I was heading their way, they were incredibly kind to give us a behind-the-scenes study trip.

Patrick, our wise and witty guide for our two-day study trip, met us at the shuttle stop, and I instantly felt at ease as he assured me he would try to get all my questions answered.

As our shuttle transitioned us from the parking lot to the Ark Encounter grounds, something deep started to stir in me. Suddenly Noah, this man who I'd been studying for months, became amazingly real. I began to feel the weight of the inaccurate Sunday school song I used to sing myself and to my own girls about Noah and his "arky." This was no vacation Bible school version of a cute little boat with animals sticking their heads out of it.

I felt incredibly small and insignificant standing next to the ark. My respect grew for the five decisions Noah made and how important it is to make those same decisions. Standing at the ramp entrance that leads to the interior of the ark, I whispered a prayer of thanks. Suddenly it was all becoming a lot clearer in my soul.

Listening to God is a decision in the midst of multiple decisions.

I'm thankful Noah went first, but it is up to us to follow when life is hard and doubt is rising.

> So faith comes from hearing, and hearing through the word of Christ.
>
> Romans 10:17

Listening When Someone Tells You Differently

One thing you may struggle with is knowing if we can really trust what we believe to be true.

Early in our marriage, Kris and I were moving into our first house. Money was tight. Stress was high. Our second baby was on the way, and Taylor, our firstborn, had been sick for a week. We kept trying to unpack boxes and freshen the stale walls with new paint, all while trying to comfort her to no avail.

She was running high fevers but had no symptoms like a cough, runny nose, or even an upset stomach. Exhausted after a long week, we made an appointment with her pediatrician, hopeful for answers.

After a few questions and a brief examination, the doctor sent us home. He told us to ride it out—it was just a virus.

It was one of those emotionally agonizing moments when your instinct is telling you one thing, but the expert is standing there saying the polar opposite.

We hadn't even made it halfway home when Taylor stopped crying, her face turned blue, and her breathing became scarce. I dialed 9-1-1 and frantically explained what was happening.

The dispatcher instructed us to head straight to the emergency room, as fast as possible. The emergency medical team was waiting for us when we pulled up.

After a series of tests, they came to us with some hard news. A condition in Taylor's urinary tract had caused an infection through her whole body. Her fever had spiked to a shocking 105 degrees, which made her body go into a seizure. A dose of IV antibiotics and a few days in the hospital would make her feel better, for now. But this wasn't something that was going to fix itself; she would need surgery.

My guess is you've had a similar experience. When something inside you told you one thing, but the "expert" standing in front of you said something else. You believed the expert, and it turned out they were wrong. And then you were sorting through all the frustrations that could have been avoided had you believed what that something deep inside you was telling you.

There will be times when you must fight for what you know to be true. Especially when it comes to the things of God.

You and I both have an enemy of our souls, whispering, shouting, and lying to us all day long. And he would love more than anything for us to follow *his* words and his ways. But remember, this is a you versus you battle. Sometimes the greatest voice of doubt is the one you allow in your head.

We have a promise from God that gives us more power than our enemy. We can call it our gut, our instinct, or our intuition, but this is what was promised to us: the Holy Spirit.

But the Helper, the Holy Spirit, whom the Father will send in my name, he will teach you all things and bring to your remembrance all that I have said to you.

John 14:26

Emotions make it hard to hear God. One of the best ways to deal with doubt is to have a character that is developed over time by a firm commitment to do what we are told by God, that is, by obedience. The presence of the Holy Spirit is a personal, living reality. His presence makes the difference between holding belief and really believing. He connects us to God as a personal presence in our lives, interacting with and working in our own thoughts.

> The Holy Spirit makes the difference between holding belief and really believing.

CHAPTER 5

A Prayer of Belief

Sometimes people ask me how many children I have, and I say, around sixteen. Only three are humans, though. Like most farms, the Fixer Upper Farm seems to have a constant cycle of animals in and animals out.

Last spring, Kris and I made the decision that our female cows—Autumn, Paisley, and Keeva—were properly grown women and ready to be bred. We had two options: 1) artificial insemination (I know, gross), or 2) rent a bull.

Three years ago, I didn't even know it was a thing to rent a bull. But it is indeed a thing.

Since we're first-generation farmers and have no idea what we're doing, we went with option two. Enter Butch, the bargain rent-a-bull. I call him the bargain bull because I had heard to breed fancy horses it can cost $10,000 or more for one round of a breeding meet-and-greet. When I found out we could have Butch at the Fixer Upper Farm for three months for only $350, it seemed like a deal to me!

Butch is a very large Highland cow. He has a beautiful gray coat and is incredibly friendly, despite his intimidating nose ring and majestic horns. And our girls (cows, not humans) were very interested in Butch as he pulled up in his red trailer. And Butch got to work right away, if you know what I mean.

Over the course of the three months Butch was with us, he did his job. Multiple times. In front of our friends who stopped by; any time I seemed to look out the window; and, of course, whenever Kennedy, our youngest daughter, was out tending to her horse. She would giggle her way back into the house eager to tell me all about who Butch was "working" with today.

We were confident our three females were all pregnant when Butch left. And we found out they make cow pregnancy tests. I'm serious! The only issue is you have to collect their urine. Like, yourself.

These were not my finest moments. Standing in the hot sun, following these cows around with a plastic cup to collect the urine, swatting flies, and waiting for them to pee. Dear ten-year-old Nicki, take anything that has to do with a classy life off your what-you-want-to-become list, because it doesn't happen.

Turns out a group of female cows is a lot like a group of teenage girls; if one has to go to the bathroom, they all do.

Finally, one evening, we timed it just right, ran up, and collected all the samples we needed. I was ECSTATIC to see all three of our cow pregnancy tests turn a bright blue color, indicating they were all pregnant.

In typical Nicki fashion, I quickly posted our exciting news all over social media, and hundreds of people chimed in with their excitement. People are kinda crazy in love with our cows; they are super invested in them. In fact, at most speaking engagements I go to, someone will come up to me and say, "I just love Autumn; she's my favorite!" Or, "Paisley is so sassy; she reminds me of my daughter." Forget the books I write, videos I teach on, podcasts I put out, and the social media posts I labor over in love for hours—people just want to talk about their favorite cow!

We left the pregnancy tests in the barn and went inside feeling so.much.joy. Three babies would be making their way to our farm, and I couldn't wait!

But the next morning, as Kennedy was letting her horse out of her stall for the day, she noticed Paisley's test went from blue to clear. I had a sinking feeling maybe I had made the announcement too soon. Sure enough, we did another test on Paisley and she wasn't pregnant.

I think I've given people social media PTSD with my announcements about barnyard babies being born on our farm. I mean, there was that time I thought our momma pig, Juliet, was about to give birth ANY SECOND. Two months later, she finally had her piglets.

And then there was that other time I thought Helen, our donkey, was pregnant for a whole year, and she was just . . . in a season of fluffy. And who could forget, just a few months after bringing Keeva home, we walked out into the field and there was a baby calf standing next to her!

But doggone it, I had done the pregnancy test this time. It was just false!

Instead of admitting I was wrong (AGAIN), do you want to know what I did? I'm so ashamed. I just went and edited the post to remove the announcement about Paisley being pregnant and just kept it about Autumn and Keeva. I thought, *Oh, in nine months, no one will even remember!*

How wrong I was.

Almost weekly someone would message me to ask for an update on Paisley, as I was posting a lot about Autumn and Keeva's pregnancies but nothing on hers. To this day, I still have people ask me what happened to Paisley's baby. I'm telling you, people are INVESTED in these cows. Lesson learned.

Nobody ever wants to admit they were wrong.

> Sometimes the courage to believe and speak belief doesn't come because we've been wrong before.

I often wonder why the courage to believe and speak belief doesn't always align in our souls. I'm convinced it has something to do with the way we've been wrong before.

And being wrong has a way to silence our ability to speak belief more than anything else, especially when it comes to listening to God. Honestly, because I've been wrong before, more times than not I just keep my mouth shut about the things of God. Because I don't want to be wrong. Not because of pride. No, it's much deeper than that.

I don't want my being wrong to cause more doubt to rise in myself or in others. I want this holy confidence I know God offers us through His presence in my life, but how do I get it and still walk in a holy humility when I don't get it right?

There is a confidence God offers each of us that comes from intentional listening efforts. But making the decision to get there isn't simple. It's going to require discipline, commitment, and, goodness, even humility in admitting sometimes we get it wrong.

The What-If of Wrong

The thing about being wrong, especially with the things of God, is that we might not ever know if we were actually wrong. From the time we are little humans we are taught that obedience brings results. Do what your teacher says, get a gold star. Put your shoes away like Mom asked, no yelling. Follow the diet, you'll lose weight.

So it's easy for us to think following what God says should also bring expected results. But I can't tell you how many times

I've seen people follow what God told them to do and there was nothing to measure their obedience by.

Missionaries who packed up their lives to live in a foreign country to serve the people there, only to be there a few weeks and then forced to leave. People who started God-inspired businesses only to not have enough customers to sustain the business. Or moms and dads who prayed faithfully for their children only to see them wander in the wrong direction.

> Will you listen and obey what you've heard, even if you don't see the expected results?

I guess the question becomes, Will you listen and obey what you've heard, even if you don't see the expected results?

This is a tension in our souls for sure. Which is why David, the psalmist, also knew the importance of asking God for clarity in his soul by praying these words:

> Search me, God, and know my heart; test me and know my anxious thoughts.
>
> Psalm 139:23 NIV

If anxiety was an issue thousands of years ago when these words were crafted by David, it shouldn't be such a surprise that anxiety is at what seems like an all-time high in our culture. Our thoughts tend to be a place where anxiety plays the game of "what-if" so loud.

What if you got something wrong about what God said?

What if you don't know the Bible like you think you do?

What if you're wrong and will miss what is right?

So many what-ifs. But what if you don't have it wrong? What if you won't miss it because God loves you too much to let that happen?

As we pursue the things God is asking us to believe, having this same posture that David had is so important. God will sift through your thoughts one by one. And He knows your heart.

A Simple Prayer of Belief

I'm not going to offer you ten ways to know for sure that you will always hear God correctly. Because you won't. The truth is, I don't think many of us are willing to admit this. But I want this ability to believe what I've heard from God with the humility to understand the process of listening. Sometimes I get it right, sometimes I get it wrong.

We do have to trust the process of the Holy Spirit. His ways are mysterious. And we are going to have to constantly counteract what we're consuming. Because I know you're not just sitting around reading your Bible all day long, having no conversations, and just sitting in silence all day. We work. We have lives. We do lots of things. And there's a lot we let in our heads and hearts.

But not all of it is from God. We have to sift through it. I'm not here to shame or guilt-trip you about your last Netflix binge. This is not a news flash; you can consume secular content and still hear from God. For sure.

However, we have to pay attention to what is God and what is not.

And so, one of the prayers I'm praying in this process of learning to listen and trust what I hear is this:

> God, if I have it wrong, show me the right way. But God, if I have it right, help me to stand still until you fulfill what I've heard.

A prayer I'm sure Noah prayed, maybe not the exact same words, but with the same heart he wondered if he heard God right.

When I pray that prayer, somehow it brings me to a place of freedom in my soul, knowing I'm surrendering it to God and asking Him for a holy confidence, but joined with the hand of holy humility.

> Listening to God brings a holy confidence joined with the hand of holy humility.

There will be times when you will feel you've heard something from God and it will be wrong. And there will be times when you feel you've heard something and it will be right. But if we don't get a hold of our disbelief, doubt, and unbelief, we could find ourselves in a position of not being willing to take a chance and listen.

It's a risk. And if we aren't willing to risk things in faith, we might be risking things to fear. Fear always wants to lead us toward failure. Fear loves to remind you of all the times your circumstances made it seem like you had it wrong. Fear wants you to stay silent, because it succeeds when you do.

But fear doesn't have to be what you listen to.

The Silence in Listening

Sometimes writing to music is helpful to drown out the noise, but most of the time I need pure silence to write. These words I'm writing to you are on a deadline, and it has been extra loud in our house lately. So I hopped on Amazon and found a solution. These headphones. They work so well, I can barely hear my fingers typing right now. Crazy and delightful.

When I need to focus, quiet is good. But when I'm home alone cleaning, or out for a walk, on a long drive, or trying to fall asleep at night, I need noise all around me. I stream podcasts, worship music, or use a sound machine all day and night.

Isn't it strange how noise can both distract and comfort us at the same time?

What sounds are you hearing right now?

I imagine some of you hear kids fighting in the background. Others of you hear the rumbling of a dishwasher or some other household appliance. And maybe even a few of you are sitting on a beach reading this while listening to the waves crashing and a faint sound of someone's radio playing just down the sandy shoreline from you.

For some of us, silence can be so awkward . . . even uncomfortable.

In the last chapter we saw God's way and word of hope for Noah. But you know what we don't see from Noah? Words. Unlike other people in the Bible—Moses, Ruth, Rachel and Leah, or even Jesus—there are no words spoken by Noah (until after the flood) we can study. That's been one of the hardest parts about learning and understanding this passage. There's no glimpse into his heart like the psalmist David gives us. And there are no prayers or comments to dissect through a word study.

With Noah, we only see this: God commands, Noah listens.

Maybe God needed us to see this silence from Noah. Perhaps one of the greatest things we can learn from Noah is this process: God commands, we obey. I want to hear what he was thinking, feeling, experiencing, questioning.

But honestly, do you know where I really struggle to have silence?

During prayer.

I realize for some of you this isn't a struggle at all. You have mastered the ability of being still and quiet before God. But goodness, this is a huge struggle for me. And I suspect also for quite a few of you.

I think I might have an idea why. . . .

If you grew up going to church and Sunday school, you may remember someone teaching you how to pray based on the acronym ACTS.

A—Adoration

C—Confession

T—Thanksgiving

S—Supplication

It's a great way to help you focus while praying, but there is no silence in this method. I can't remember a time when someone taught me the importance of being silent before God. Most of us have never been taught about the spiritual discipline of silence.

First, the word *discipline* sounds yucky to most of us.

Second, why would God ever just want us to be silent before Him?

If you struggle with the word *discipline* because it makes you feel like you're being sent to the principal's office because you did something wrong, we could instead use the word *habit*.

Spiritual disciplines or habits are practices we find used in the Scriptures to help us have growth in our life. They are an action that helps us grow closer to God. Silence is considered one of the eight spiritual disciplines we can find examples of in the Bible.

I wonder if you are anything like me that in my moments of fear and worry, silence is the last thing I feel like I'm supposed to do. I need to process, talk it out, and then, maybe then, I'll be ready to listen to someone else.

But if we're going to defeat this mountain of doubt in our lives again and again, silence is going to have to become part of life. We're going to have to learn to get comfortable with it. Because silence before God is a source of strength.

> Silence before God becomes a source of strength.

Here's something neat you may not have noticed before. The word *listen* contains all the same letters as the word *silent*. It's what's called an anagram.

Because I know silence before God is important for my soul, I'm trying harder and harder not to pray just to be heard, but to pray with the intent to listen. But again, I don't always get this right.

What the Experts Say about Silence

Silence isn't just a spiritual discipline. In fact, for years now, psychologists have been trying to tell us to quiet our lives down. According to psychology.com, these are some of the benefits of silence:

Stimulates brain growth.

Just two minutes of silence can lower your cortisol (stress) levels.

Periods of silence throughout the day can help you sleep better.

Silence can help get your creative juices flowing.

Your immune system can get stronger by regular practice of silence.

The awareness of yourself and environment becomes clearer in silence.[1]

God shows us how He speaks through silence in the Scriptures (Luke 1:20). Jesus models silence for us (Mark 1:35).

The experts tell us silence can improve our lives. Our brains work better with periods of silence. So why has our Christian culture not embraced the silence in the listening? And why is silence so hard for some of us?

Simply put, I think noise has always been a tactic of the enemy. But I'm not here blaming the devil for everything wrong in our lives. We make choices. And noise is often a choice.

> "God speaks in the silence of the heart. Listening is the beginning of prayer."
> —Mother Teresa

I realize there are seasons and moments of our lives when noise is inevitable. Raising kids is noisy. Working in environments with others is noisy. Walk outside and you will hear noise. But my question and challenge is, What do we do in the moments when it's possible to be quiet? Those first few moments you are awake in the morning or before you fall asleep at night. The break in between this and that.

Do we scroll mindlessly through social media? Read something to keep our mind busy? Play music or a podcast? Call a friend?

There is power in noise and there is power in silence. It's up to us to decide which one we let speak to us more. God is found in the silence more often than not. Mother Teresa said this best: "God speaks in the silence of the heart. Listening is the beginning of prayer."

End-of-Chapter Challenge

Set a timer for ten minutes and be completely silent and ask God to speak to you in the silence. After the ten minutes are up, journal what you experienced. What was hard about it? What was easy? What did you feel? After a few times of doing this for ten minutes, bump your time up a few minutes longer and keep trying to build this discipline into your life.

CHAPTER 6

Pruning Doubt

When we first moved to the Fixer Upper Farm, it was a bit of an eyesore. Weeds six feet tall. Broken windows. Snakes swimming in the broken-down pool. And so many bushes that needed to be trimmed way back.

We have girls. And girls are great and can do anything; I'm a total believer in that. But my girls? They aren't exactly the farm-help type.

So I asked my friend Wendy if her son, Griffin, would be interested in being our farmhand for the summer. We promised a decent paycheck for a teenage boy, a pool to jump in whenever he needed to cool down, and three girls to cheer him through his projects for us.

Griffin was amazing. He did everything we asked, faster than we could have ever done it, and we really trusted him. We kept giving him more and more to do. Kris and I had several conversations with Griffin about the various bushes on our property that needed to either be trimmed back or cleared out altogether. I thought we were all on the same page with what needed to go and what needed to stay. But I think we may have had some miscommunication about our rose bushes.

Imagine the shock on my face when I pulled in one afternoon and saw Griffin waving hello to me as he mowed down the only things salvageable—these beautiful, blooming, mature rosebushes, completely down to the stub. I almost screamed, "Nooooooo!"

Because when you live in a fixer upper, very few things look beautiful from the get-go. Those rosebushes were it.

We didn't make a big deal about it with Griffin. I knew it was honest miscommunication. But I thought those bushes were goners.

The past two years, as I've walked through so much loss, I have felt very much like a bush who got run over with nothing left to bloom. See, this could be the cheesy part of the message where I tell you that the way I'm blooming now looks so much better than it did before. But the reality is, it's still so ugly.

Staying rooted instead of running is always a risk.

It still kinda feels like there's a lawn mower running over me again and again. Sometimes I feel like there's more that has to go than needs to stay at this point. I know this pruning, this reshaping, is for my good.

But sometimes I'm scared. Am I ever going to get this? Will these mountains of belief actually move? Am I hearing God? Will I embrace silence?

If we don't want our disbelief to turn into unbelief, everything that has caused disbelief to stir in us has to be pruned back. Way back. All the way to where there is almost nothing left.

Those rosebushes didn't come back the next summer. But the summer after that, they did.

And their blooms were beautiful.

Thankfully, the roots had matured enough to not be completely pulled up by the lawn mower. Likewise, there is much of this process that will feel like a risk to you and me. Trust in the midst of questions is always a risk. Belief when it feels unbelievable is always a risk. Staying rooted instead of running is always a risk. Being humble enough to admit things need to be removed from within us feels like a risk.

Pruning doesn't mean we forget the hard, the bad, or the pain. It means we cut it back far enough to allow something better to grow again.

Because will we really change? Will anything be different this time?

Deciding to listen, especially with the pruning of our souls, could feel like one of the hardest things God could ask us to do.

But every season of our life, even seasons of growth, provides the opportunity to cut some stuff back. What is God pruning in you? And like the silence, will you allow this change?

The Perspective in Pruning

The final piece of instruction God gives Noah for the ark is to make sure it has a window and a door:

> "Make a roof for it, leaving below the roof an opening one cubit high all around. Put a door in the side of the ark and make lower, middle and upper decks."
>
> Genesis 6:16 NIV

This door will be significant to remember in the next section of the book and when we discuss the window. But I want us to notice here the perspective the door on the ark offers us. Noah's ark is a representation of what God does for us today. He's our hiding place. Our saving place. Our shelter from the storms of life that will come. The place that changes pruning to power, doubt to belief, and floods to faithfulness.

The door to the ark reflects God's way for us to have access to Jesus.

> So Jesus again said to them, "Truly, truly, I say to you, I am the door of the sheep."
>
> John 10:7

Like everything else we're talking about in this book, Jesus is a decision. But not a one-and-done decision. It's an everyday decision to "open the door" and "come into the ark."

After God had given Noah the instructions for the ark, God revealed the "pruning" that would come from the flood.

> "For behold, I will bring a flood of waters upon the earth to destroy all flesh in which is the breath of life under heaven. Everything that is on the earth shall die."
>
> Genesis 6:17

Feels harsh, doesn't it? But remember, we can see this as God's meanness or God's mercy. Because the next few verses tell us everything that God *wasn't* going to destroy:

> "But I will establish my covenant with you, and you shall come into the ark, you, your sons, your wife, and your sons' wives with you. And of every living thing of all flesh, you shall bring two of every sort into the ark to keep them alive with you. They shall be male and female. Of the birds according to their kinds, and of the animals according to their kinds, of every creeping thing of the ground, according to its kind, two of every sort shall come in to you to keep them alive. Also take with you every sort of food that is eaten, and store it up. It shall serve as food for you and for them."
>
> Genesis 6:18–21

This ark would be Noah and his family's refuge in the middle of hopeless and hard. And the fact that God didn't totally give up on humanity is a continued hope for those of us living in a world that seems so similar to Noah's. A new beginning was coming for Noah and the world, but to get there, it would be hard.

Doubt surely surrounded this situation. Possible doubt from people watching Noah build the ark, doubt about his warnings, and doubt about this new beginning ahead. Was this the best way?

I've wondered if Mary, Jesus' mother, asked this same question as she watched her son die on a cross: *Is this the best way?*

And I know you and I have asked it too, because hard things make us question. *God, does it have to be this way?*

But with God, the reality of hard always holds the perspective of hope. It's what we choose to see and what we choose to hear.

The Radio Message

After the trying situation I shared in chapter 4, with Taylor's need for surgery and the doctor who wouldn't listen to us, we found a new doctor and moved forward with the care Taylor needed. A few months later, with a very pregnant stomach, I arrived at the hospital for Taylor's surgery at an ungodly early hour.

Taylor's surgery went well, and we met her in the recovery room, where everything was anything from smooth after that point.

The anesthesia made something fierce come out in her, and she began kicking and screaming. Taylor was only two years old, and to this day I don't know how she knew this phrase, but every time a medical professional would try to do anything like give medication or take blood, she would scream, "Don't agitate her!" (*Her*, meaning herself.)

83

She became known as the bossiest big-word-using two-year-old on the seventh floor.

The stress and screams weren't beneficial for an eight-month-pregnant woman. In fact, I started having contractions. And eventually the nurse told me to go home or I would be going from floor seven to floor eight to deliver a baby.

With tears in my eyes, I closed the door to Taylor's room and left Kris in charge for the night. As the elevator took me down floor after floor, it felt like the weight of each floor went down with me.

My keys turned the ignition to my car on, but it felt like I was on autopilot.

Hopelessness has been something I've struggled with for a lifetime.

It's not depression. I've experienced seasons of that. It's not sadness. I've had that too. It's like this doom and gloom cloud that seems to hover over my soul, making me forget that I have this God who is the God of hope.

> The reality of hard always holds the perspective of hope.

To distract my hopeless thoughts, I turned on the radio.

I turned the volume up to hear what this woman on the radio was saying. She shared a devastating experience about losing a child who was very young. After her heartbreaking memory about what had happened, she started to share how the baby had impacted an entire community.

Grown men found themselves at the altar of their church, weeping and turning to God for their families. People came to know the name of Jesus through her story. And even though the baby lived only six months on this earth, her story and her name lived on.

The baby's name? Hope.

I had pulled into the garage, a weeping mess, and was sitting in the silence for a moment when something happened.

God was speaking something to me. A name. For this baby I was carrying. Her name was to be *Hope*. I felt like we were supposed to name her this to be a constant reminder that even though this season was hard and there would be more hard seasons, hope was always near.

The only problem? Well, I'd never actually had an ultrasound to determine the baby's gender. So how was anyone, including my husband, ever going to believe me?

The next morning, for the first time in months, I awoke with hope. And even though I had zero proof of what had happened to me that night, I had my belief. And I needed to tell someone.

I called Kris and excitedly told him everything that had happened. He was exhausted from being with a screaming child all night and didn't come close to meeting my excitement expectations. He only mumbled something about getting to the hospital ASAP.

My hope-filled attitude accompanied me all the way back to the hospital. I got off the elevator with a little skip in my step—well, as much skip as an eight-month-pregnant woman can have. But there she was, right there to greet me: doubt.

A woman who looked like she had lived an abundance of life was mopping the floors. She seemed like one of those wise souls you should probably listen to any chance you get. I smiled as I walked past her. "Mmm, girl. That is some boy you are carrying in that belly."

My legs stopped. I turned around and asked for clarification. She went on to inform me about the many baby-momma bellies she had seen in her lifetime, and she was sure a boy was in mine.

I didn't know what to think or say. Why was this random woman telling me this?

Doubt started to rise.

Doubt Didn't Win, This Time

We made it through Taylor's recovery process, and then on a cold November morning I started to feel intense pain in my back and that sense it was baby-delivering time.

We pulled into the parking lot of the hospital, and I looked at Kris and assured him, this baby was a girl and her name was going to be Hope, and God would be with us through all the hard things.

I believed it with all my might.

How on earth we rolled into the hospital delivery room with a nurse holding our chart that stated we were having a BOY is still a mystery. I panicked. How did the doctor know that? Had she seen the early ultrasound that stated it was a boy?

The nurse checking us in wanted to believe me. But they believe charts.

I was in so much pain that I needed an epidural and an epiphany.

For the next six hours, with every single person that walked into my delivery room, I demanded their guess on the gender of this baby.

Boy.
Boy.
Boy.
Not sure.
Boy.
Boy.
Boy.

I couldn't believe it. I was so mad. I started to wonder, *That night in the car, when I knew I heard God, did it really happen?*

My fury turned into furiously pushing. I had to know if this baby was a boy or girl. My faith was depending on it.

The doctor, knowing my frazzled name-for-a-baby story, stood at the edge of the bed and asked me to focus. She assured me that if it was a boy, it was going to be okay.

One push turned into ten, and then she and the nurse gasped: "It's a GIRL."

Not an eye was dry in that entire maternity suite.

Truly, Hope had come. And I realized I wasn't crazy. I saw I could be a woman who walked with God. He would speak to me in my silence, and I would listen.

I hold on to the moment God so clearly showed me Hope's name quite a bit. But listen, it's ONE moment in a gazillion in my lifetime. There have been more moments that have looked the complete opposite. Ones that left me feeling like I am not able to hear from God at all.

Maybe you're not at the place where you've experienced anything like this in your life either. Maybe this all sounds like a bunch of foolish talk to you. Maybe you think you don't have a name for your situation to hold on to.

But you do.

The Name to Hold On to

When I toured the replica ark at the Ark Encounter, I noticed even beyond the actual building of the ark, there were so many interior things to think through. Rooms for food storage, a water supply system, a way to feed all the animals each day, sleeping quarters for Noah and his family, and some types of cages for animals to be kept in. Until I held the realization that there were upwards of seven thousand creatures coming onto this ark, I think I just always assumed, like those cute storybook pictures reflect, that the animals were all on board just hanging out together.

Even though on the Fixer Upper Farm we allow all our animals, except the chickens, to roam around together, it couldn't be that way on an ark. It would be chaos. Loud, smelly chaos.

I even wondered if God would have brought the animals on board and then graciously allowed them to go into a deep sleep. We don't see in Genesis 6 God telling Noah exactly how long he would be on the ark, but we do see Him give instructions to gather up food for his family and the animals. So out went the sleeping theory in my mind.

How did Noah know how to execute these somewhat vague instructions God gave him?

Well, the same way you and I execute the things God calls us to today: the Holy Spirit.

I realize all of us reading through this may not have had the same experience when it comes to understanding the Holy Spirit. It feels like a very mysterious thing, and I think it should. As we've already talked about, there are things about God on this side of eternity that won't make perfect sense. The Holy Spirit sometimes feels very unexplainable. No matter where you find yourself on the Holy Spirit spectrum, let's see a few things the Bible reveals to us about who He is.

The Holy Spirit allows us to have access to incredible things: wisdom, understanding, gifts of healing, faith, miracles, prophecy, and the ability to pray in a supernatural language God understands (1 Corinthians 12:1–11). The Holy Spirit is also a comforter (Acts 9:31) and a helper (John 14:26). And while all of that sounds so neat and amazing, the Holy Spirit also has another job: to convict, or we could say, prune.

To listen to God well, we need to hear the easy things just as much as we need to hear the hard. We can't have just one. That's not the full picture of what our process with God is like. And it has to be the same as we study the Bible.

We need to hold both Truth and the Spirit. God speaks in so many ways, and we need the Holy Spirit to reveal things to us. It's how you can read a verse a dozen times and then on the thirteenth time, it does something different to you. It's why you can have moments like I did—in a car listening to a story on the radio—and hear God speak. And I'm sure the Holy Spirit is how Noah could execute those big plans for an ark and thousands of animals to enter.

Quite a few people think the Holy Spirit first appeared in the New Testament book of Acts, when He descended on the followers of Jesus on the day of Pentecost (Acts 2). *Was the Holy Spirit even around in Noah's time?* The answer is yes. He is first mentioned as the Spirit of God in Genesis 1:2. Later, in places like Judges 14:6, we see that the Spirit "rushed" upon Samson. There are many mentions of the Spirit before Pentecost.

God, Holy Spirit, and Jesus have always worked together on our behalf, speaking in different ways, but with the same purpose.

I wish I could tell you that when you hear God speak, it will be something amazing like my Hope story. But it could be something totally crazy, like our guy Noah heard. Or something totally different, a pruning of sorts. But regardless, may it be with us as it was with Noah. . . .

Noah did this; he did all that God commanded him.

Genesis 6:22

To Rise Above the Doubt

CHAPTER 7

Doubters Gonna Doubt

W hat would it mean for you to believe in who God
created you to be so much that any voices of doubt
from others would simply go in one ear and out
the other? In theory, it sounds great, right? I think we would
all love to be incredibly confident people who just do what we
are made to do. All without ever letting in a voice of doubt to
discourage us.

Most of us wouldn't want to admit this, but others' opinions
do matter to us.

One of the most common questions I receive is, "How did
you get started with speaking and writing?" The truth is, I
didn't have a huge support system to begin this calling.

Of course, I had some incredible friends who cheered me
on. But there have been people who filled my mind with doubt
seemingly every opportunity they had. And I'll never forget one
night, around a dinner table, when the voice of doubt almost
won. . . .

Before I wrote or spoke for Proverbs 31 Ministries and other
venues, I taught a Bible study in my home and then later in

our local church. The study grew pretty large, and I was honing in on this thing that gave me so much life, teaching the Bible.

I had heard about a conference that Proverbs 31 Ministries put on called She Speaks. It's an incredible place for speakers and writers to come and develop their calling. At the time, the conference also provided an opportunity for new speakers to join an evaluation group to get some honest feedback about the way they presented a message.

This sounded both terrifying and thrilling. But also, it felt like the only way I would know for sure if I was cut out to work on becoming a public communicator. I know now that's not true, but in that season, this conference was everything to me.

Kris and I had just come out of a long season of financial loss during the recession of 2007. I was working as a preschool music teacher, and he was working as an electrician for a small company. We had purchased a tiny house that, of course, needed a lot of fixing. And we were just barely getting by.

As I researched things, the She Speaks conference felt far out of reach financially. So I took a risk and put out publicly on my blog the fact that I was raising money to attend the conference. Incredible things started to happen. My original Bible study girls all chipped in as much as they could, and a few hundred dollars came off my cost. For the first time in a while, I had hope.

But a few days after writing the blog post, I was sitting at a dinner table with people I had known for years. One of them brought up the blog post. Her sharp words stung: "I would never give you money to attend a conference like that."

Several others at the table nodded their heads in agreement, and my stomach sank as I caught Kris's eyes. He returned a sympathetic look and we hurried through the dinner and left as quickly as possible.

I cried on the way home and almost deleted the blog post, vowing never to try to do anything toward writing or speaking again. But Kris, my calm and steady support system, talked me off the quitting ledge, again.

Soon a generous donation of several hundred dollars came in. We sold a few things at a yard sale. My parents chipped in, and before I knew it, I was packing my bags and heading to the She Speaks conference.

This conference became the launching pad for where I am today. Had I given in to the doubt I received around the dinner table that night, I don't know if I'd be sitting here writing these words to you right now in this capacity.

This is the part of the message that is hard to share because I honestly hate this.

I wish I could tell you if you walk with God and listen to God, people will jump up and down and throw you a following-after-God faith parade. But it's quite the opposite. In fact, in the beginning stages of your process, you will probably have more people who don't believe in you than those who do.

There's something, across the world, where you have to prove yourself before people believe in you. Part of me understands, because I've had a lot of people come my way over the years telling me that they, too, want to speak and write.

I will often spend hours pouring into them, telling them everything I know they can do, and then, crickets. They do nothing with what I share with them. And then five years later, I hear from them again that they're finally ready to go around that mountain again. It's frustrating, but I never want to be someone who makes someone feel like I don't believe in them. I'm sure you've had similar situations when you've wondered if you should keep investing your time into someone.

But sometimes we become naysayers without even realizing it.

Your Naysayers and You

While I have had my fair share of naysayers in life, I must confess I have been my own naysayer and I've been a naysayer to others. These are not fun things to admit. I'm a big believer of learning to look at ourselves first before we look at the rest of the world with our critical eye. Because if we're not willing to vulnerably rise above our own faults, we should never expect others to.

My oldest daughter has felt something from me I'm not proud of. She's a dreamer, much like I am. She wants to change the world for the good. I've always said her bossy ways were executive leadership material, and I still believe that. She has and will continue to do big things with her life.

> If we are not willing to vulnerably rise above our own faults, we should never expect others to.

But it's super easy to slip into analytical-critical mode when she brings me a big idea. It's not that I don't believe in her big dream, it's that I see the obstacles in her dream. I want her to think through things so she doesn't fail.

However, multiple times she has said she feels like I'm squashing her dreams. I remember my mom making me feel the same way when I said things like I wanted to become a nurse and move to a developing country. Or the time I told her about the brilliant business idea that was sure to bring in thousands of dollars in one week. I'll never forget her sarcastic response, "Really? Okay . . ."

Neither of those things happened. And my mom was right about some things. But still, I hated it. I just wanted her to say, "Go do it!" And a lot of times, she did. But I vowed never to make my kids feel that way.

But gosh, here I am, doing the same thing. Honestly, how do we bring reality AND a rah-rah-you-can-do-it cheer to someone's assignment from God when it feels really far off? I haven't quite figured out that rhythm. But I'm working on it.

At the end of the day, all I really want my daughter to know and believe is that I am for her. But there's a difference between people who are for us and want to help us see what we need to see and the people who are just against us.

The main difference is the people who are for you are the ones who stick around. They are curious about your life. They ask questions. They may not always make you feel amazing, but they think you're amazing.

Those people at the dinner table that night? I haven't spoken to either of them in years. And the last time I did, it was very short. They care nothing about my life, calling, or assignment. And that's fine. We don't need everyone to believe in us. But we need to believe in ourselves and we need to believe in others.

My daughter just came to me and told me another big idea she has. I swallowed all my doubts and told her I thought it was the best idea ever without one side-eye look. That's what she needs from me in this season. I heard her. I'm listening. And as she transitions into adulthood, I'm trying to do this mothering thing better.

In your own process of learning to rise above the things that feel hard in life, you will have ideas. You will have dreams. You will have naysayers. And you will have dream defenders. But it will be your decision to rise above the doubt that floods your mind about who you are based on what others say, and what you're becoming despite others' judgments of you.

Here are a few tips to help you navigate through naysayers:

1. Consider not sharing the process until your confidence matches the calling.

Just because God calls you into something doesn't mean you have to share it with anyone. This can be a holy-sacred place with just you and Him until the time is right to share it with others. Our adoption is one of these places for me. I'm not ready to share this process with the world and let everyone's opinions in. The ones I have let in are enough. I know this is a very sacred place God is calling our family, and when it's time to share this story, He will show us.

> But when you pray, go into your room and shut the door and pray to your Father who is in secret. And your Father who sees in secret will reward you.
>
> Matthew 6:6

2. Surround yourself with positive voices.

I know the people I can trust with my God-dreams, desires, and hopes, and I know who I can't. Not sure who to trust? Try sharing something small, like, "I think I'm going to try to walk every day this week," and see what kind of reaction you get. Do they immediately turn things back on them by saying something like, "That's a big goal. I once walked every day for a week, and it didn't turn out well for me." If they turn your goal into something negative about their life, they are not your people. Find the people who say, "Text me every day you take a walk so I can cheer you on."

> Whoever walks with the wise becomes wise, but the companion of fools will suffer harm.
>
> Proverbs 13:20

3. More actions, fewer words.

Sometimes I feel like we spend more time telling people about the thing we want to do more than doing the thing we want to do. Your behind-the-scenes will eventually reveal the reality of how much you're willing to put into this. I have a motto: Keep your head down. Work hard. And prove them wrong by your outcome.

> I have fought the good fight, I have finished the race,
> I have kept the faith.
>
> 2 Timothy 4:7

4. Take what you need, leave the rest.

We can't just reject every ounce of feedback that sounds even the least bit critical. There are times we should listen to what feels like negative feedback, to see if there's anything we need to look at differently. This is a very humble yet guarded place. Like, if I'm walking around with toilet paper dragging on my shoe after visiting a public bathroom, I want someone to tell me. It doesn't always feel good to have someone point out something I need to see, but those who are willing to see what they need and let go of the rest often go the furthest. They don't let an opinion shape them. They're humble enough to say, "Show me what you see."

> Iron sharpens iron, and one man sharpens another.
>
> Proverbs 27:17

This is hard stuff. And we are often the hardest on ourselves. We can be the loudest naysayer in our own lives. We have to decide to come into the places wherever God invites us with a holy confidence that He called us there. Where He calls, we go. Because that is where faithfulness is found. This third decision is one we will need to make every single day: to rise above the doubt.

Decision Three: To Rise Above the Doubt

The Best Command: Come

We're about at the halfway point of this book. Let's recap some of what we need to remember about Noah. First, Noah walked closely with God. He listened and obeyed. He received his ark-building, animal-gathering, humanity-saving assignment. For over 120 years, Noah worked faithfully on building the ark. He rose above the culture, the fear of man, and the impossible, doubt-filled feelings this assignment surely brought.

And now, he's arrived at the place where all the work is completed. And God gives him one last command: *come*.

> Then the LORD said to Noah, "Come into the ark, you and all your household, because I have seen that you are righteous before Me in this generation."
>
> Genesis 7:1 NKJV

In the previous verses, it felt like God was angry (which He was), and this all felt harsh (it was harsh, but also hopeful). But this last command—"Noah, come into the ark"—feels like a random gush of a cooling wind on a hot summer day. Unexpected. Kind. Refreshing.

This is one of those places in the Bible where I needed to go to someone smarter than I am and ask what exactly was meant by this verse, especially that word *come*, because I was confused as to why some versions of the Bible use the word *come* and others *go*. This is what my theological friend David Abernathy said:

The word for "come" also has the meaning "go" (you see the same in Greek). It means to move from one place to another, and whether it is translated "come" or "go" depends on where the person is relative to the speaker. If the person being addressed is supposed to move toward the speaker, then it's translated "come." But if it's just a matter of moving from one place to another and the location of the speaker is not in view, then it is translated "go."

Only KJV and NKJV translate "come"; all others translate as "go" or "enter." "Come" suggests that God is in the ark and is inviting Noah and his family to come in. But it's really just

100

a command to go into the ark, although since God is present everywhere, it is sort of like going into a sanctuary, of sorts, because the ark is certainly a sanctuary for life, where all life will be preserved.

God doesn't force us, He invites us.

It's a lot easier to enter a hard place when we know God has commanded it. This part of Noah's process reminds me of Romans 8:31: "What then shall we say to these things? If God is for us, who can be against us?"

All the doubts, all the fears, all the critical words spoken over Noah, they are about to be washed away by one last command. God also gives you and me this command today: come. The ark represents the place of salvation and security for us today that we find in Jesus.

But unlike Noah, who was commanded to come, the command for you and me looks like an invitation. God doesn't force us into this. He invites us, and it's up to us to accept the invitation.

After this last command, one of my favorite scenes from the Bible appears in the text. If I could have one day at any point in history to re-live, it would be this one: *The animals entering the ark.* The text doesn't offer us a lot of details about how this really went down. But let's see how much we can figure out.

Two by Two?

I'll admit, as a first-generation farmer, I've been a little delusional about our animals. I assumed if you loved an animal, fed it well, and took care of whatever it needed, it would stay put. In its area. And be content.

Oh, how wrong I've been, multiple times.

I could write an entire book titled *The Fixer Upper Farm Barnyard Escapes.* Featured on the front cover would be our expert escapees Fred, the miniature donkey, and Princess Lolly, the potbelly pig. Those two have somehow figured out how to get out more than anybody else.

I missed the greatest escape ever executed on the Fixer Upper Farm. I was out of town when Kris called me and said, "You won't believe what happened." Those words are a frequent way we start our conversations, but this time? It was pretty crazy.

Fred had somehow opened the gate (read: most likely someone forgot to lock it) in the barn and led all the animals out one by one. Everyone. The pigs. The cows. The horse. Fred and his girl-friend, Helen. EVERYBODY. Wherever Fred goes, they all follow.

Kris was coming home from picking one of our girls up from school and was pulling down the long gravel road when he had to do a double take to make sure he was seeing what he thought he was seeing. Our cows, Autumn and Paisley, were standing in the creek on our neighbor's farm. Fred, Helen, and Princess the horse were happily grazing in the front yard. Oh, and the pigs had gotten into our neighbor's field.

It was QUITE an escape, and it could have ended badly. It took Kris several hours to get everyone rounded up and back to where they belong. Eventually, everyone was safe and sound.

Because I know how hard it is to "round up" animals, I can't help but wonder what this process of loading all these animals into the ark was like. I'm sure it required patience and a plan. These were the details God gave Noah:

> "Take with you seven pairs of every kind of clean animal, a male and its mate, and one pair of every kind of unclean animal, a male and its mate, and also seven pairs of every kind of bird, male and female, to keep their various kinds alive throughout the earth."
>
> Genesis 7:2–3 NIV

This is where we see one of the most common misconceptions about the account of Noah and the ark. The animals didn't *all* actually come two by two. Notice in the previous verse, it says the words "every kind."

For basic study purposes, most likely some of the types of animals that came seven by seven were every kind of bird, every kind of oxen, every kind of sheep, and every kind of goat.

The ones that came only in pairs would most likely have been pigs, horses, Freds and Helens (wink), and other similar animals.

Today, there are many "kinds" of dogs, birds, cows, etc. We can't say for sure how many "kinds" of goats, cows, horses, etc., there were during Noah's days. But we know based on the God-given dimensions for the ark it was a lot more than we might think.

On this side of eternity, we will never know if Noah had begun corralling the animals months before, or if they just all showed up on the same day or over a few days.

What I do know is Noah and his family had to help these animals get onto the ark and into their secured location. Which for untamed animals had to take patience and innovation—things I've learned all farmers need.

The animals didn't just show up in front of Noah's clipboard of room assignments and go where they were told. There had to be a plan and patience with the plan.

As you accept God's invitation to come, you will also need patience and a plan. You will need patience for yourself and for others—the naysayers who show up for you, and the naysayer you can be to yourself. There will be doubt that others bring

Like Noah, we need patience and a plan.

you, the doubt you bring yourself, and the doubt you bring to others. We're not exempt from any of it. But we always have the chance to make the decision to rise above the doubt.

Somehow Noah got all those animals onto that ark. Somehow you will also do the hard things. Because God is never a naysayer. And He believes in you more than anyone on this earth ever could. He knows you have it in you. He knows you're the one He can look from heaven and point to and say, "That's the one, the one who walks with me, listens to me, and rises above all the doubt." He knows because He invited you into this. And you said yes. You're in it.

CHAPTER 8

Please, God, No More Hard Things

Please, God, no more hard things.

    Have you ever found yourself whispering those words to God? It was a frequent prayer in my season of being flooded by doubt.

Just three weeks after my brother died, I was sitting on the couch one morning, beginning my day with a cup of coffee. Kennedy was home from school for the day, and one of her morning farm chores is to let her horse, Princess, out of the barn. She's very responsible, so I wasn't surprised to see her slip out the door while I sat and drank my coffee and began planning my day.

If you were sitting in my living room that day, you also would have known something wasn't right as her boots loudly stomped back up on the porch after being out for just a few minutes.

She opened the door screaming that something wasn't right with Princess, and I needed to come quick. I grabbed my phone, threw on my boots, and ran out as fast as I could. Princess is an older horse, and she would often lie down in her stall at night. I wondered if her arthritis was bothering her.

But this morning, she wasn't getting up—at all.

I quickly called our horse trainer, who instructed me to get her up as soon as possible and take her out into the pasture and get her walking around. And to call the vet immediately.

I was able to get Princess's harness on and we got her to stand up and walk outside. At first, she seemed like maybe she was just having some arthritis pain, but then very quickly she started to fall over and roll back and forth. Again and again and again.

I knew it was bad.

I called the vet, and wonderful as he is, he was stretched really thin that morning and was at another emergency and couldn't get to us for at least two hours. I had no idea what I was going to do with a horse in this kind of condition for two hours.

I prayed. I asked the Lord to give me strength to comfort this horse in a way only He could. It would become the longest two hours of my life. The only thing I knew to do when Princess would fall and roll in pain was to sing to her and rub her forehead to calm her.

In this stressful moment, the only song I could remember the lyrics to was a song from elementary Sunday school, "He's Got the Whole World in His Hands." I hadn't sung that song in years, and yet somehow my soul needed to sing it right then. To know that every moment of life on earth was held in the hands of God was the only thing comforting at a time like that.

Eventually Kris came back home, the vet arrived, and help was there. We were no longer alone.

But our vet wasn't fluffing around with a diagnosis when he got there. He said it was colic and she had to be put down.

I couldn't believe I had barely said good-bye to my brother, and now this? It was too much. And can I be honest? It still feels like too much during a season like that.

Please, God, no more hard things, I whispered.

Princess had a look in her eyes. She was tired. She was old. She had lived a good life. She loved us. And the Fixer Upper Farm was her home. But she was in pain. So Kris signed a piece of paper that gave the vet permission to allow Princess the ability to exhale one last time.

They say the breath of heaven feels like the wind between a horse's ears. I don't know what the breath of heaven is like, but I can imagine it's something as powerful and beautiful as the wind sweeping over your face on a long horse ride.

Princess taught us so much. She was a pain, moody, and just sassy most days. Her size intimidated me, and she knew how to get her way. But she was our first horse. And in her eyes, we could see that the love she had for us was never doubted.

As her eyes closed for the final time, grief overwhelmed our souls so much we couldn't even stand. We sat beside her for quite a while, letting our tears fall on her face.

I know you're wondering, What on earth do you do with a thousand-pound horse that dies? We had no idea either. But the vet told us about a local organization that would come out for a donation and bury the horse on our property. We called them and they quickly came to help us.

From my home office, in my navy blue wingback chair, I can look out into the field and see the place Princess is buried. She's right next to our chicken coop, which is currently filled with new life: baby chicks. An ironic reflection of farm life for sure.

I know it was better to have loved Princess for two years than to have never loved her at all. But hard things during hard seasons make us want to forget that it was worth it.

Loss hurts—the ending of what was. And sometimes it makes looking ahead feel incredibly hard.

I'm not sure I believe the old saying that *time heals all wounds.* But I think time can be a gift to our wounds that eventually become scars. And other times? It can feel like salt on our wounds.

Nothing but Waiting

I wonder if at any point in Noah's process he cried out, *"Please, God, no more hard things!"* Could it have been during the 120 years of building the ark? I can only imagine the things that went wrong with the building process. The challenges. The fingers cuts by saws, splinters from wood. The aches in muscles and backs from lifting. Or the tiresome mental state of being responsible for building such a massive structure. Those things that made him feel like he was failing and needed to whisper *"Please, God, no more hard things."*

> Time does not erase our wounds, but time allows them to eventually become scars.

Or did this cry of his heart to ease this assignment come after Noah had completed the final task of loading these animals up and his family had entered the ark? That part alone had to be exhausting emotionally and physically.

And what about the final warnings he gave to his friends, neighbors, and even his extended family? That had to feel hard as well. Noah was carrying grief in knowing what was coming before anything was even lost.

Something that isn't super clear in the Scriptures is whether others were given the *opportunity* to enter the ark. The command from God was that Noah, his wife, his sons, and their wives would enter the ark and be saved (Genesis 6:18), but was there even a chance for anyone else? There are so many things we will never know while we're here on this earth. And trust me, I've already booked my appointment in heaven with Noah. *I have questions.*

But there were a few more hard things that needed to happen before the flooding would begin. After everyone was loaded into the ark, the waiting would begin. And waiting is often harder than working.

Because I know all too well how kids (no matter their age) can be with their parents, I can't help but picture an eye roll or two from one of Noah's sons. "Okay, Dad, we're all here, loaded up, now what?"

Noah's calm voice probably assured them there was a plan: *"Now, we wait."*

"For in seven days I will send rain on the earth forty days and forty nights, and every living thing that I have made I will blot out from the face of the ground." And Noah did all that the LORD had commanded him.

Genesis 7:4–5

Those seven days of waiting before the flood was to begin must have felt like an eternity of waiting and wondering.

Waiting for it all to begin.

Wondering what it would look like for the world as they knew it to end.

Waiting for God to speak again.

Wondering if they were doing the right thing.

Waiting for others to join them.

Wondering if they would be alone.

Waiting for a flood.

I'm not sure why God waited seven days to start the flood. But what we must remember is the fact that the timing of God is never hurried by the impatience of man. No matter how many times I've pleaded with God about His timing, we don't get to change the timeline of God.

That's one of the greatest struggles with obedience: time. It's easy to wait on God when we're waiting on a same-day miracle.

But I have found the greatest things God has done in my life have come from a long season of waiting. Faithfulness is not built on momentary agreements and arrangements with God. It is built through days, weeks, months, and years of showing up with expectancy, hope, and belief.

Sometimes, like with Princess, our horse, we have to wait two hours for relief to show up, which can feel like an eternity. Sometimes we have to wait seven days for a flood to begin, which can feel like an eternity. And sometimes we wait a lifetime for something we may never see fulfilled until we reach eternity.

Rising above the timeline of man to trust in the timeline of God won't be simple. We will feel alone. It will feel incredibly hard. Doubt will meet us there, for sure, but once again, it's our decision to rise.

When Everyone Isn't In

What was everyone else in Noah's community doing around this same time as Noah and his family waited for the flood to begin? Well, living their lives.

> For as in those days before the flood they were eating and drinking, marrying and giving in marriage, until the day when Noah entered the ark.
>
> Matthew 24:38

You know, often when we feel like God has called us into an assignment, not only do we want people to support us with their words, we also want people to support us with their actions. We want them to believe with us, stand with us, and wait with us. But what do we do when it seems like we are in this thing completely alone?

We've already talked about the naysayers, but what about the ones who are just completely silent?

I meet people all the time who say things like, "If I just had more people to help me, I could do this." And yes, there is a real thing in our lives called *capacity*. We can only do so much on our own. We need other people. God didn't create us to do life alone. And I do believe at the right and appointed time, God will send people to help us fulfill what He's asked us to believe Him for.

> If we are waiting for someone to come alongside us and usher us into obedience, we might be waiting at the end of that aisle for a lifetime.

But often while we're waiting, we're looking at the rest of the world and start wondering, *Hello, is someone coming to help me do this?* And then we face the reality, like this process was for Noah, that most of the world around us is still living their life. *As they see fit.*

If we are waiting for someone to come alongside us and usher us into obedience, we might be waiting at the end of that aisle for a lifetime. So the question becomes, Will you rise above the doubt that comes when doing this alone?

The belief you hold in God is important. But the belief you hold in yourself is important too. I'm seeing too many of us walking around with a doubt about ourselves—doubt that comes from feeling alone in all this.

Noah had to have people helping him build the ark, and most likely, because people are people, someone said something like "Are you sure you want to do it *that* way? What about *this* way?" Experts were most likely all around Noah trying to boss him around with their ideas.

But where were they now? Why did they still not believe what Noah said to be true?

Noah did what God commanded him to do. He was able to push past all the doubt, loneliness, fear, and negativity around him. It didn't matter what others said or thought about him when it came to his obedience, because ultimately, he built the ark and got on it.

This doesn't mean Noah's soul was not impacted by the opinions and words of others about what he was doing. That old saying, "Sticks and stones may break my bones, but words will never hurt me," is one of the greatest lies of our lives. Words hurt. However, we can be impacted by the opinions of others, isolated in our actions, and not become defeated to the point that it causes our own disobedience.

How to Stay Positive When Negative Runs Toward You

I don't know where you fall within the need to have others affirm what God is doing in and through you. I don't know what waiting has done to your soul. But man, it feels good when someone pats us on the back and tells us we're doing a good job. Maybe sometimes you think, *If I could just have that "one" person to tell me they believe in me, this would be easier.* I want you to know, I understand. As a words-of-affirmation love-language girl, sometimes I look at my husband and say, "Just say something nice to me."

He always laughs and says something silly like, "You married a really great guy." But when Kris Koziarz gives me an authentic word of affirmation, I will replay it in my head three thousand times.

> Hurtful words do not have to be the words we allow to define us.

But I have to also be careful when someone gives me harsh criticism, because I tend to replay that in my head three thousand times too. Often the things we need, like words, will come in the form of a weapon against us.

Waiting on words of affirmation from others can also become a place of disobedience in our lives. So how do we stay positive in our hearts, minds, and souls when it feels like so much negativity is being run toward us? Whether from others or from ourselves, it's there, so what do we do?

Here are a few things I've learned to do that help:

Be brave.

I give you permission to be kind, but also to be brave enough to stand up for yourself. It takes courage to decide to obey God. And there will be doubters, whether through their silence or their criticism. Sometimes this is as simple as blocking someone on social media. Other times it may require a face-to-face conversation. We don't have to be rude or critical back. In fact, it's hard to rise above the doubters by not sinking to their level.

But there is a place of kind-bravery in you. I know it's there.

You can and will be brave enough to not allow someone's opinion or lack of affirmation over you, your dream, or your God-given vision determine your outcome.

Give it some time.

Negativity, whether from others or from yourself, will make you want to give up on this process. Remember, the ark wasn't built in a day. And this incredible thing God is building in you won't happen in a day either. We are so impatient and want things here and now. Give yourself the time to grow and to grieve what you need to grieve, and when you're ready, go. One of my go-to verses about time is Ecclesiastes 3:11:

> He has made everything beautiful in its time. Also, he has put eternity into man's heart, yet so that he cannot find out what God has done from the beginning to the end.

I remember praying this verse as a little girl, thinking it would somehow make me pretty one day. I would look in the mirror and see all the things I hated about myself, but somehow, I believed one day God would make me beautiful and I would feel beautiful. While I still don't love many things about myself and the way I look in pictures, I now understand the process of God pruning something in us to make it beautiful. And it has nothing to do with an outward appearance. It's a heart reflection.

Noah has taught me that time is the test of our hearts. Whether it takes one year or a hundred years, how will we remain faithful through the long and the short?

Remember who you don't want to be.

This process can also teach us who we don't want to become. I remember during the release of my first book, *5 Habits of a Woman Who Doesn't Quit*, I became consumed by the opinions people had about that message. For the most part, 99 percent of people loved the message. But goodness, the 1 percent that didn't? They were harsh and they were loud. The sad thing is, some of those negative voices were other writers. Their opinions seemed to hurt the worst.

> Everyone has something to teach us, and sometimes it's simply to remember who we never want to be.

But after that book-release season, I vowed to never speak negatively about another writer's work. Just recently, I was in a group setting where someone started saying negative things about an author. I took up for her. Even if I agreed with what was being said, a negative person is not who I want to be.

Everyone has something to teach us, and sometimes it's simply to remember who we never want to be.

We don't want to be the kind of people who wouldn't get into the ark with Noah if given the opportunity. We want to be people like Henry Blackaby describes in his book *Experiencing God*—people who find where God is moving and join Him there.

More hard things came in this process for Noah, and more will come for you and me. But today is a really good day to decide, *This is worth it*. All of the highs and all of the lows. Who you are becoming today will determine who you will be tomorrow. Make the decision again and again to keep rising above the doubt.

CHAPTER 9

Enough Is Enough

I sense by the time these words make it into your hands, the term *Covid-19* might feel a bit like a cuss word to your ears. All of us have grieved something Covid-19 caused us to lose. And words like *quarantine* and *stay-at-home orders* became part of our vocabulary during this season.

But here's something interesting as it relates to our process here in this book. Noah and his family were the first quarantined people we know of in humanity. Not only that, they were the first ones to be given an order to *stay in place and shelter.* The first ones called out to separate themselves from the rest of the world. And they were the first ones to understand the depth of what happens when a warning has been given about the fragility of life both spiritually and physically.

But instead of a president, governor, or local authority, the one who called the stay-on-the-ark order? God.

And the LORD shut him in.

Genesis 7:16b

This one-half of a verse is filled with so much that we have to pause to truly understand. After everyone was loaded into the ark, the door was closed. But not by Noah, not by anyone in his community or family, but by God. Some Bible scholars believe this is an example of God's grace—Noah not having to be the one to close the door.

Can you imagine having to be the one to make the decision of closing the door for the final time?

As I've watched leaders during Covid-19 struggle with when to close and reopen doors to stores, restaurants, and even churches, I can feel the weight of what they've carried in these decisions. No matter what they decide, someone won't agree with it. They've had to have a perspective beyond opinions, politics, and the fear this virus has brought. They've had to rise above a lot of noise and make decisions despite what all their doubts tell them.

Perhaps this was the greatest moment of relief, grace, and mercy for Noah—the door closing.

As the flood waters began to rise, I think about the sounds outside of the ark that they must have been able to hear faintly. The water rising, people screaming, perhaps even people running toward the ark, begging Noah to let them in. The angst Noah must have felt as he exhaled for the first time in this long, hard, trying process as the door closed. Only to inhale the next reality: Destruction was coming.

Friends. Family. Co-workers. Neighbors. Playmates from childhood. The person who sold them their groceries and supplies. They would all be gone in a matter of moments.

Once the door was closed, that was it. The hard thing, perhaps the hardest, was done. And it wasn't man's responsibility to do the hardest part.

This is the promise to hold tight to in the midst of hard things. We do our part, but God does the hardest. He never expects us to carry the weight of what it means to believe Him above all our doubts. Trust often feels like the hard thing . . . in the midst of the hard thing. But I have to also remind myself that God has a habit of doing holy things in the midst of hard things. The problem is, we normally only see the hard.

There's More Where that Came From

Write a book on overcoming doubt and you will be flooded with opportunities to doubt or to believe.

To say that I've been flooded with doubt about what it's going to take to come out of this current season more than just surviving would be very correct.

I keep looking for that Bible verse that says following God means things should be easy, simple, and clear. But as hard as it is to say, there is no such promise from our God.

Often during hard seasons, I just want to escape. Go somewhere. And just forget about all the hard things. But often when we're in the midst of hard things, there's nowhere to escape.

But these country roads out here by the Fixer Upper Farm have provided a place of respite and reflection during this stay-at-home season. Sometimes country roads and Tim McGraw blasting through your speakers are all a soul needs to exhale for a moment.

> God has a habit of doing holy things in the midst of hard things.

I found myself on one of these drives after a day filled with hard things. I rolled the windows down, looked at the roads glowing with light from the sunset, and just told God how incredibly sad I was.

My joy, my strength, my hope . . . it all felt like it had been stolen from me, and doubt about everything was flooding me.

When emotions like this begin to stir inside of us, we have to remember where they come from. None of those feelings of hopelessness come from God. I'm reminded of the words Jesus himself said to the enemy,

> Then Jesus was led up by the Spirit into the wilderness to be tempted by the devil. And after fasting forty days and forty nights, he was hungry. And the tempter came and said to him, "If you are the Son of God, command these stones to become loaves of bread." But he answered, "It is written, 'Man shall not live by bread alone, but by every word that comes from the mouth of God.'" Then the devil took him to the holy city and set him on the pinnacle of the temple.
>
> Matthew 4:1–5

If Jesus had to remind Satan where everything in our lives comes from, we should take note.

That day when I was driving down those roads processing all the things, I sensed what I needed to do: "Tell the enemy, there's more where it all came from."

Sometimes I just need a practical way to break out of the pit life can toss us in. Our words matter in this battle to rise above the enemy's attempts to sink us lower and lower.

If Jesus had to remind Satan where everything in our lives comes from, we should take note.

I spent several minutes that day reminding the enemy of my soul where my hope, joy, strength, and blessings came from.

I say those same words to you today. Whatever you feel is lost, sinking, or disappearing, tell the enemy there is more where it all came from. We're all trying to run from these emotional floodwaters, but maybe we just need to stop running and decide to rise on them. As we accept what feels lost, we rise toward the next beautiful thing God has for us. Take a minute and . . .

Tell the enemy, there's more joy where your joy came
from. (Psalm 28:7)

Tell the enemy, there's more hope where your hope came
from. (Romans 15:13)

Tell the enemy, there's more strength where your strength
came from. (Psalm 46:1–3)

Tell the enemy, there are more blessings where your blessings came from. (2 Corinthians 4:17)

The one thing I want to caution us about with this process
is the reminder that we should never give the enemy more attention than we give God and His Word. The enemy doesn't
deserve it. And I forget this all the time. I'm thankful for the
patience and promise of God to always meet me where I am
in this growth process with Him and not where I wish I was.

As the door to the ark was closed, enough was enough. And
in your life, as you enter this holy, sacred place with your God,
you must also allow God to close the door—enough is enough.
You get to decide how many times a day you will choose to rise
above the doubt. You get to decide when enough is enough.

After I spent a few minutes reminding the enemy where
everything in my life came from, I turned off my beloved Tim
McGraw and put on the most powerful worship music I knew.
When that drive was over, I felt better. My circumstances didn't
change during that drive, but my soul did. And that's where
real change begins.

The Water Rose and Rose and Rose

Over two hundred cultures across the world have an account
of the flood. Many veer from the biblical account, but there
are a lot of common threads among each account. The main
common thread is the flood covered the entire world. For forty

days and forty nights, rain poured from heaven and came up from the earth.

> The flood continued forty days on the earth. The waters increased and bore up the ark, and it rose high above the earth.
>
> Genesis 7:17

Unlike a tsunami that pushes a huge surge of water into land and causes flooding, this was more likely a gradual but very steady increase of water.

> The waters prevailed and increased greatly on the earth, and the ark floated on the face of the waters. And the waters prevailed so mightily on the earth that all the high mountains under the whole heaven were covered.
>
> Genesis 7:18–19

Even while this storm surrounded the ark, inside was a place of safety but also work.

It's not like Noah and his family were lying around watching Netflix for forty days and forty nights. There were thousands of animals that needed to be fed, cared for, and looked after. There were still meals that needed to be made for their family.

If Covid-19 made me realize anything about my family, it's how much my people eat. I felt like all I did was grocery shop, cook meals, clean the kitchen (or yell at someone who DIDN'T clean the kitchen), and plan the next meal.

I don't know who did all the cooking on the ark, but Lord bless them because cooking in a dark, rocky ark had to be quite a way to cook.

When I studied at the Ark Encounter, I appreciated the creative visuals showing how things might have looked for Noah and his family on this ark. Most likely they each had a room they slept in, a kitchen, a living/gathering room, and they had to be innovative with lighting. Because according to the Scriptures, there was only one window on the ark, so it must have been super dark.

Having fire on a large structure made of wood also provided challenges, I'm sure. But somehow, they were able to have lanterns and safe fires that allowed them to cook and see.

Remember, they didn't have to steer the ark, so there was no stress in trying to make sure they were going in the right direction. God oversaw that. But everything inside the ark was all their responsibility.

I keep thinking about what could have been some of the emotional challenges with Noah and his family on the ark.

The Koziarz crew has many different personalities, and Covid-19 brought out the best and worst in all of us. I really had to decide what was worth battling over: dishes "accidentally" left in the sink? Not worth the fuss, I just put them away.

In a "normal" season, I wouldn't.

However, rude tones and harshly spoken words to each other? I wouldn't tolerate it. My girls had some ugly feelings about each other most days, and when they chose to share them? Phones were taken away, extra chores handed out, and warnings upon warnings given. Enough was enough with that.

Any family in close quarters, with nowhere to escape, will have challenges. For sure, Noah's family got on each other's nerves, fought over whose turn it was to feed the lions, and wondered if everyone was pulling the same weight around that ark. I'm sure things had to constantly be talked through and processed, and boundaries had to be set in place. And when the arguing got out of control, I'm sure Noah's wife said something like *"ENOUGH IS ENOUGH!"*

I'm sure they also found games to play, songs to sing, and their favorite ark-quarantine snack, and they probably would often gather around to listen to the accounts of the faithful followers of God before them that Noah would share. After all, the entire history of humanity was on that ark now.

This third decision we see in Noah's account—to rise above the doubt—is one we must make again and again.

As we come into our own ark of sorts through Jesus, there is safety, security, hope, and protection. But we must remember that coming into this hard place with God leads to the holy things of God. And there will be things that need to be left in the water. There are relationships that cannot come with us as we rise. There are mindsets that can't stay. And there are things on the other side of this process we have to trust in because we cannot see it yet.

The Significance of Forty

Before we wrap this section of the book up, there is one more concept we can't skip over. That is the significance of the number forty in the Bible and how it relates to this process of us learning to make the best decisions while being flooded by the hard things.

The number forty signifies new life, growth, transformation, and change. But it can also represent a time of trial, testing, or judgment. The number forty appears around a hundred times in the Bible. Here is a list of a few things in the Bible that relate to the number forty:

Jesus fasted in the desert for forty days (Matthew 4).
Moses was forty years old when he was called by God
(Acts 7:23).
The battle between David and Goliath lasted forty days
(1 Samuel 17:16).
The Israelites wandered for forty years in the desert
(Numbers 14:1–35).

Isaac was forty years old when he married Rebekah
(Genesis 25).

The people of Nineveh had to repent for forty days
(Jonah 3).

And obviously, for Noah, it rained for forty days and forty
nights. But this won't be the last time we see forty appear in
the account of Noah.

I'm not saying there's a magic formula to the number forty,
but there is a spiritual and biblical significance to it. And I've
always been taught that whenever we see something repeated
in Scripture, it should make our ears perk up and we should
listen closer. The fact that the number forty is mentioned so
many times in the Bible should make us lean into it.

I can't tell you exactly what God wants to do through the
number forty in your life, but I believe if there's something
significant in the Bible about it, there's something significant
for you. Instead of trying to guess what it means, how about
we just follow some of the examples in the Bible?

There's something coming up in this chapter I really want
you to do. A challenge. Can I be honest for a second? I can
picture some of you sitting behind these pages, wanting to turn
the page to the next chapter and skip over this part. Because
you have enough going on. You really don't want anything else
"to do" in your life. And you aren't convinced there is anything
significant to this for you.

If you turn to the next chapter, I will never know. But if
you are willing to give this a try and see what God wants to
show you through the significance of forty days in your life,
keep reading. I have such an expectancy for you to experience
something special with God. And hey, shoot me a message on
your favorite social media outlet and let me know what you
decided to do.

Remember, the hard things lead to the holy things. Let this challenge be something that is actually challenging to you. Seek the hard, find the holy.

Find Your Forty-Day Challenge

I can't tell you exactly what you should do for your own forty-day challenge. I would encourage you to pray and ask God to reveal to you what would help you the most through this struggle with doubt, since that's what we're working on in this book. I have found that when I tackle one struggle at a time, I'm more likely to find victory than when I decide to tackle everything in my life that feels messed up.

Because I know that sometimes we need something to help get our wheels turning to figure out what to do, here is a list of possible things you could do for your forty days:

Pick one book of the Bible to read slowly.

Fast from social media or TV.

Decide to not look at your phone for one hour after you wake up.

Buy a forty-day devotional book. There are a ton out there, but one of my favorites is *Draw the Circle: The 40 Day Prayer Challenge* by Mark Batterson.

Take a prayer walk.

Set a timer for fifteen minutes and sit in silence.

Read the same verse each day.

Create a new morning routine.

Pray one prayer.

Pick one of these things and commit to doing it for forty days. Fill in this box that follows, and when you're done, I

encourage you to share it with a friend or two, or even post it
on your own social media.

My forty-day challenge start date:

My challenge:

What God showed me:

To Remember Who Is in Charge

CHAPTER 10

What Goes Up
Must Come Down

Turns out car rental companies have an inconvenient rule for forgetful people. Apparently, if your driver's license is, oh, say, *expired*, they won't let you rent a car. I never needed to know this rule. Until I did.

I was in a bit of a pinch when I arrived for a speaking event in San Francisco and was informed by an extreme rule-following car rental associate that my license was expired. She let me know there would be no rental car for me. I had some anxious thoughts because I was very far from home, all alone, and had an event that was counting on me to show up.

But my personality type is one to always have a plan B. Which with driving scenarios is always Uber.

I pulled up my Uber app and plugged in my destination and waited to be matched with a driver. According to the Uber estimated drive time, the event I needed to get to was one hour and fifteen minutes away from the airport. That's a long and pricey Uber drive, but there was no plan C.

Uber informed me a kind soul named Cesar, in a blue Toyota Camry with a 4.8-star rating, would be there in approximately four minutes to pick me up.

Perfect.

Cesar the Uber driver arrived, loaded my luggage, pulled up the address of where we were headed, and that's when things got slightly complicated.

I should also mention, Cesar didn't speak much English. But he knew enough to exhale deeply as he looked at his phone and say, "Oh. Yikes. This no good where I take you." I could tell he was debating whether to unload my luggage and let someone else from Uber come get me. But my time was limited to get to the event, so I promised him a REALLY good tip if he got me there. I mean, how bad of a drive could it be?

Reluctantly, Cesar took off.

The first half of the ride was fine. No issues except a little car sickness. I had totally forgotten California has mountains. BIG MOUNTAINS. Whenever I think of California, I think of beaches or people strolling Rodeo Drive.

But apparently, we were headed right into the mountains, which must have been why Cesar was reluctant to take me. So up the mountain we started to go. I noticed that according to the GPS, Cesar missed a turn, so I said, "Um, Cesar, I think you need to go back that way."

Cesar sighed, agreed, and pulled the car over to the side of the road. But instead of turning around at the next exit, he just straight-up backed up on the side of the road. Real fast. And then whipped the car around the turn.

At this point, my stomach was feeling more than queasy and my nerves were getting a little unsettled. I reached for my calming essential oil roller and put it on every inch of my body I could.

Cesar started saying all kinds of words I couldn't understand as he turned down a road called Bear Creek Road, which I have forever renamed Death Creek Road.

As we made our way up this long, windy road, Cesar got quiet. His hands seemed sweaty. And the look on his face was one of pure fear. I got really nervous. I honestly thought he was going to drop me off on the side of the road. I kept envisioning myself calling the event coordinator from the side of Death Creek Road and asking her to come pick me up. Not a great first impression.

After many more twists, turns, and almost flips off the edge of the mountain, my nerves were shot. Cesar turned down the final road, and I breathed a huge sigh of relief. But then I realized, Cesar was not okay.

In fact, Cesar was . . . crying. And not just a tear. He was sobbing.

I think he said, "NEVER AGAIN. NEVER."

I tried to comfort Cesar, but it was too late. So I reminded him I was going to tip him really well. And then I started to cry because I felt so bad for him. After all, he had to drive back down the road. I wasn't sure Cesar was mentally up for this. I thanked him, hugged him, and gave him a big tip and a five-star review on Uber.

I didn't see anything on my Twitter news sources that night about an Uber driver dying on Bear Creek Road, so I'm sure he was totally fine.

As I've wrestled with doubt over the last few years, it's seemed a lot like that Uber drive up Bear Creek Road.

Sure, sign me up. I want to be a faith-filled follower of Jesus. Oh, wait. This isn't what I thought it was going to be. It's actually really hard. And Lord have mercy, I'm not gonna make it. I don't want to do this anymore.

And then, I get a chance to exhale at the top of the mountain only to realize Newton's Law also applies to me: *What goes up, must come down.* It can be just as hard coming down the mountain as it is going up the mountain.

Eventually, we have to make the decision to go up and go down. There is a strength within us we don't even know is there until we go. God is not going to push you up or down the mountain of doubt. You will stay on those rising waters as long as you need to. He meets us in His mercy no matter where we are in this process. But the decision to trust His plans for both the up and the down resides within us.

God Doesn't Forget

One of the most basic human needs is to be seen and valued by others. I've been guilty of walking closely with a friend through the beginning of an uphill battle but unintentionally withdrawing after a period of time has passed. When people walk through an extended season of pain or hardship, life stops for them, but it continues to go on for the rest of the world. I've had to become intentional to not forget to step into people's pain with them and yet to not let my mind forget what they are experiencing.

Being valued by others doesn't necessarily mean being elevated, but it does mean being remembered. Being seen by others doesn't necessarily mean being popular, but it does mean we feel like people know we exist. Being remembered and recognized is important to us whether we are willing to admit it or not.

When we don't feel seen and valued by others, it becomes incredibly easy to start to believe God doesn't see or value us. In extended seasons of pain, loss, grief, or hardship, it's easy to wonder, *God, have you forgotten me?*

As Noah and his family remained on the ark for days and weeks that turned into months, I'm sure they wondered when God was going to act on their behalf again. Did He still see them? Did He hear their frustrations? Why was it taking so long?

As we turn the page into Genesis chapter 8, we see one of my favorite parts of this passage:

But God *remembered* Noah and all the beasts and all the live-stock that were with him in the ark. And God made a wind blow over the earth, and the waters subsided.

Genesis 8:1 (italics added)

In doing research for this book, I came across a video from a man who is an atheist. He was trying to prove God doesn't exist and how absolutely absurd this part (Genesis 8:1) of the Scriptures was to him. He said in the video he couldn't believe anyone would want to believe in a God who would want to destroy the entire earth and then forget about Noah and his family on the ark.

If we were going to just read the verse as is, I could understand his point. But that's not what this verse means.

It's the exact opposite.

This word *remembered* here means God is about to take action on Noah's behalf. We can see several places throughout the Scriptures (we dig into this in the companion Study Guide for this book) where the word *remembered* is used in this capacity and then God does something on the person's behalf.

It's like remembering someone's birthday, or anniversary, or something important to that person. You take the time to call, text, send a card, or buy a gift ahead of time. Or remembering an appointment: You get up on time, get dressed, make sure you arrive a few minutes early (or scoot in at the last second, like me). You're there. You didn't forget. It just wasn't time to do anything before that specific day.

God remembers. Action is about to take place. It is time for the flood waters to recede.

What goes up must come down.

While we think the uphill climb is the hardest part, I found out a large number of hiking accidents actually happen on the way down. Spiritually speaking, I would say a lot of us are strong enough to get to the top, but coming down can be a different story.

Send in the Wind

Wind is this weird thing we want and don't want, right? Everyone wants the wind when it's hot outside; it makes things better. But no one wants it when it's cold; it just makes things worse. But sometimes wind is necessary for something beyond our comfort or discomfort.

In Genesis 8:1, we see God is "remembering" or *taking action* to bring Noah, his family, and all the animals out of the ark. The way He's taking action? By sending a wind to push the waters back.

> And God made a wind blow over the earth, and the waters subsided.
>
> Genesis 8:1b

This was not a blow-out-the-candle-on-the-cake type of wind. Or a wind that feels really good while sitting on the beach on a hot, sunny day. This had to be a massive force. One that inside the ark they surely felt.

Throughout the Bible, there are other places God uses the wind to bring His action. In Exodus 14:21, God sent a strong wind to part the Red Sea. In Mark 4:39–41, we hear the disciples say even the wind obeys Jesus. In Acts 2:1–21, the day of Pentecost, the Holy Spirit blew in like the wind. These are just a few places wind is mentioned in a significant way.

Wind is invisible, yet we can still feel it. We have no control over the wind. It blows where it wants to blow, which is very much what it feels like to be dictated by doubt. And yet, wind can also be a picture of change as we allow the Holy Spirit to move, like wind, through our souls—pushing the doubt away until our feet stand on firm ground again.

This place in the text brings us to our fourth decision we can make when life is hard and doubt is rising: to remember Who is in charge.

Decision Four: To Remember Who Is in Charge

We know the storms of life will continue to come. But I think we often confuse "in charge of" and "in control of."

God has been and always will be sovereign over everything. God has the plan from beginning to end. But God is not controlling us in the steps we decide to take. We are the ones in control of our actions, our words, our belief, our process.

Think about God like a coach.

The coach has the team's plan. He knows what they need to do to win. He gives them instructions. But ultimately it is up to the team to decide if they will follow the plan, the wisdom, and the instructions they have been given.

Noah had the command and the plan. But there were a lot of unknowns in his process.

We don't know if the ark just hovered over the mountains and then, as the waters receded, it gradually settled onto new territory, or if suddenly there was a bang or a jerk and the ark suddenly stopped moving because it had run into the mountains. Regardless of how it happened, the storm was eventually all over and the waters started receding.

There had to be many conversations on the ark about what life would look like once this was all over. I'm sure there were many comments from the family crew. "Come on, let's just open the door and see what's happening!" It had been nine months since the beginning of the flood, and anticipation had to be building.

If Noah had forgotten who was in charge of this assignment, he could have very easily taken the game into his own hands. If he opened the door and climbed out of the ark before it was time, he could have put himself, his family, or the animals in danger.

But Noah remained patient and stayed in his process with God. Eventually, it was time to discover if their seclusion on the ark was indeed over.

The way he would find this out? Birds.

> At the end of forty days Noah opened the window of the ark that he had made and sent forth a raven. It went to and fro until the waters were dried up from the earth.
>
> Genesis 8:6–7

If the First Time Doesn't Work

The raven was up first. It flew back and forth over the land, according to Genesis 8:7, until the waters dried up, but it didn't return to the ark. Next, Noah released a dove (Genesis 8:8–9), but the dove couldn't find a place to rest, so Noah brought it back into the ark and let his family know it would be another seven days before he would try to send the dove out again.

I'm sure that update didn't go over well.

I would've been sending that dove out EVERY DAY to see if today was the day! When I feel restless, it's so easy to start to take things into my own hands—thinking there must be a better, faster way. Doubt often brings this restless knock to our doors.

I also wondered, when I was studying this, why God didn't just tell them when it was over? Perhaps it was a mysterious part of God's plan that He would allow them to figure some things out for themselves.

Haven't we all had those days when we wish we could have one phone call with God so He could tell us what to do? We don't want options. We don't want to figure this out. We just want to know, *God, what are you doing?*

What if Noah got frustrated and gave up after sending the raven out? And what allowed him to have the patience to try again with the dove?

> God's pace and God's plan are not ours to decide.

My friend Rachel Ridge is a fellow donkey lover; she sent me a beautiful print I hung just outside my home office door. It's a little donkey with a quote that says, "Above all, trust the slow work of God."[1]

I love this piece of art hanging outside the place I do most of my work. I constantly need to be reminded that God is in charge. His pace and His plan aren't mine to decide. It's so true. Most of the deepest, holiest, soul-changing things don't come from these big, huge, fast moments. It is a slow process.

And sometimes, I don't send the right thing out the window. I have to try again and again.

I feel like I've been praying for years for this doubt to leave me. I feel like I've wanted to get to the top of this mountain and settle my soul in a place of safety and security for what seems like forever. Maybe if I had obeyed some of the commands I look back on and see God gave me, I wouldn't still be rising in these waters. I'd be settled, landed, and ready to step out.

> God's in charge of the plan; I'm in control of my obedience.

But Noah didn't give up on what he was "sending out the window." Each bird was a sign of his faith. Ultimately, what was going out that window? Faith in the plan.

God's in charge of the plan; I'm in control of my obedience. Say this again and again until it digs down deep into you.

In the ups and the downs, we can still trust Him by bringing our process into His presence every day. Here are a few practical ways to do this:

1. Call out the things that feel out of control.

Most controlling behavior comes from a place of fear. Simply admitting things feel out of control is a really simple way to resettle into a place of faith.

Try praying this: *God, today this situation feels out of control. But I know you are in charge and you have a plan. Help me to not grab hold of this situation and help me trust you.*

2. Challenge your reactions.

When you know better, you should do better, right? But we are creatures of habit. And doubt is unfortunately a habit that leads to us needing to be in control. When things feel out of control, challenge past reactions with new, healthier ones. Do the opposite of what fear tries to convince you to do.

Try praying this: *God, help me not do what I normally tend to do. Help me see a new way—your way. Guide me, Holy Spirit.*

3. Change your language.

I'm a huge believer that we must be so careful what words we allow to come out of our mouth. Faith-filled words are not fake; they are holy. We need to repent from words we've spoken out of fear and not faith.

Try praying this:

Jesus, I don't want to speak words of fear based on a need to control. Forgive me for the times I have. Holy Spirit, remind me of this confession and help me to speak words of faith.

There's still so much for Noah to teach us about staying under God's plan and not making our own plan when things feel out of control. But for today, know you are doing a good work with God. Rest your soul in this place today: God is in charge of the plan, I'm in control of my obedience. The more you remind yourself of this, the stronger you will become. See you in chapter 11.

The Controlling Thing About Control

I would guess that most of you reading these words would say you are NOT a control freak. Maybe only a few would be brave enough to raise your hand and admit, "Hi, I'm _____ and I'm a control freak." But most of us would shake our heads no. We do our best to follow all the friendly non-control-freak rules.

I would say the same: *not a control freak*. But honestly, who wants to really admit they're a control freak? If there is one place where I know for SURE I could be defined as a control freak, it's when driving.

If I sat with a therapist long enough to understand this battle, I'm sure they would uncover that my real need to be in control when I'm driving goes all the way back to when I was in middle school. An accident with a semitruck that fled the scene after pushing our tiny car off the road shook me.

Whenever someone else is driving, I feel very anxious remembering this scene. Kris and I have had many arguments in

143

the car, because it's hard for me to relax when he's driving. I feel like I constantly have to be looking and reminding him of danger. He doesn't really care for this. So honestly, most of the time, I do the driving when we're going somewhere.

The thing is, I know I can control what I do while I'm driving but that I cannot control what others do. So if an accident is going to happen because of someone else's mistake, it's going to happen.

The illusion of control makes me think that if I'm driving, we are safer.

I'm sure if you think about it, there's something in your life you feel the need to be in control of.

Maybe for you it's not driving but it's the need to be in control of your finances. Constantly checking and rechecking your bank account. It makes you feel safe to be reminded of what you have. Or maybe it's a need to know where people you love are all the time. If you have an app like Life360, you are constantly aware of the location of others; it makes you feel safe to know where they are.

> Doubt wants us to believe that if we don't feel safe, we're not in control, so we should do whatever is needed to take control.

And honestly, isn't that the feeling we are all craving when we are becoming controlling . . . *safety*?

We just want to know everything is going to be okay for ourselves and the people we love.

But the illusion of control is where doubt tries to swallow us whole. Doubt tries to convince us no one can be trusted— it's not worth it to believe something can be okay beyond our own doing. And doubt wants us to believe that if we don't feel safe, we're not in control, so we should do whatever is needed to take control.

We're going to have to define what it means to feel safe as we trust God.

Does it mean that we will be rich and never have to worry about money? Will we never have something frightening happen to us? Will our loved ones not die young? Will we never get sick? These are just a few of the questions around trust I think we toss in our heads and hearts. And the thing is, most of us who think rationally know the answers to those questions. Yet we still wonder, *God, is it safe to trust you?*

When we are in between the problem and the promise, it becomes incredibly easy for doubt to convince us it's time to take things into our own hands. But it couldn't be more wrong of a time, because we're so close to the breakthrough. We're so close to seeing the promise fulfilled. And we're so close to seeing the fruition of God's plan.

When You Don't Stop Taking Things Into Your Own Hands

Just a few years ago, I said one too many yeses in my life. I said yes to working almost full time. I said yes to speaking more, which meant more traveling on weekends. I said yes to book writing. I said yes to being a volunteer at church, and I said yes to all three of my girls being in different activities. All while knowing full and well God had shown me my capacity and it was time to back off some things.

I couldn't let anything go. I just knew I needed everything. But have you ever known full and well you were supposed to *not* do something, and you did it anyway? Not much has changed in the human heart since Eve found herself in the garden next to that tree of fruit (Genesis 3).

Before I could realize the effects of my disobedience, I had frustrated co-workers, a frustrated family, a frustrated editor, and my own soul was beyond frustrated. It was a storm of chaos I couldn't stop.

Finally, one afternoon, I arrived home after a long, trying week. I knew I was supposed to resign from my staff position at Proverbs 31 Ministries, and I found myself overflowing with emotions. I had been on staff for several years, and, honestly, it was one of the highlights of my life to get to help build our online Bible studies. It led to incredible opportunities. Nothing in me wanted to step down from that position.

But I couldn't do it all anymore. I was dropping balls left and right. My life was overflowing but my soul felt so empty. Disobedience will do this to a soul: make us miserable until we move in the right direction.

> Disobedience will make us miserable until we move in the right direction.

I'll never forget the next Monday morning after a weekend of letting the reality of my resignation settle into my soul. I sat in Melissa Taylor's office (the director of our online Bible studies at Proverbs 31), and through tears, I looked at her and said, "I can't do it all anymore. I'm dying inside."

She began to cry with me, because that's just who Melissa is. She weeps with those who weep and rejoices with those who rejoice (Romans 12:15). We began to make plans for me to officially resign. But I hated every second of it. I was mad. I was sad. I was disappointed. Sometimes obedience hurts. And that's how I felt in that moment—deeply hurt. Not by her or anyone at Proverbs 31, but by myself. I didn't trust God because I wanted to control it all.

We must be brave, bold, and faithful to do the hard things. Obedience is the walking out of our trust in God.

Two weeks after my official resignation, I was at a speaking event in Virginia when my phone started blowing up with texts and phone calls. They were all about my mom. She had been in a car accident we soon learned was caused by a stage four brain tumor.

My mom was given six months to live.

In an instant, I knew God was asking me to lay every bit of it down and take care of my mom during this crisis. More painful obedience.

There were a lot of layers to that process for me. And as each one was peeled back, it got harder and harder.

I canceled speaking events. I made a hard phone call to my agent, Meredith, and confessed I wasn't in fact Superwoman and had to let my publisher know the book, which I had just resigned from my position to finish, needed to be paused.

Hard as it all was, I exhaled, thanking God that someone else had already stepped into my position at Proverbs 31 and I wasn't needed anymore in that capacity.

Those six months with my mom became the most defining six months of my life. Again and again I was reminded God is in charge. He has the plan. But it's my process, my actions, my obedience that matters. Had I continued with everything on my plate, I wouldn't have been able to be there for my mom.

It is safe to trust God even when it hurts.

> It is safe to trust God even when it hurts.

Do you think you'll be one of those people at the end of your life who will look back and think, *I have no regrets?*

I hope so. I'm always so inspired by those types of people. But if you look back and think, *Gosh, I wish I would've surrendered some of my control here and there,* you're in good company.

I don't want you to think we have to stay stuck in this place, though. While we cannot change the past, a beautiful thing happens when we realize the results of taking things into our own hands again and again: We make the decision to stop.

I don't know that any of us truly realize in the moment the root of control is unbelief. When life gets hard, some of us fade into the background and check out. And some of us reach for anything we can control.

But there's a better way, and Noah is about to show us.

Between the Problem and the Promise

After the raven and the first dove were released, Noah had another idea and the faith to send out the dove *one more time*.

> He waited another seven days, and again he sent forth the dove out of the ark. And the dove came back to him in the evening, and behold, in her mouth was a freshly plucked olive leaf. So Noah knew that the waters had subsided from the earth.
>
> Genesis 8:10–11

I want to be careful to not stretch this text too far from its meaning. As I've mentioned several times now, the Bible doesn't give us a lot to work with on Noah. But I wondered if there was a connection between sending out the raven and the dove. Ultimately, the dove is the one that brings back the sign of hope.

The raven would have been considered an unclean animal, so there would have been only two on the ark: one male and one female. It was a risk for Noah to send out the raven.

And sure enough, it didn't come back, but we know it didn't die, because did you ever hear of the old, creepy movie *The Birds*? Ravens are VERY alive today. I'm sure someone thinks they are lovely birds, but not your girl here. Thank you so much, Noah, for saving the sketchiest birds of them all.

Still, Noah took the risk in sending out the raven.

Sometimes what we send out the window the first time in faith isn't the right thing at the right time. We need to regroup, not give up, and dig our heels in a little deeper and try again. Belief is a risk. Trust is a risk. Faith is a risk. But if we don't take the risk, we might miss the chance.

The dove is a very different type of bird than the raven. It was considered a clean animal, so more than one pair made it into the ark. Doves are referenced in the Bible as a sacrificial animal (Leviticus 1:14; 12:6) and sometimes seen as the symbol of Israel (Hosea 7:11; 11:11). My favorite reference to the dove is found in Matthew 3.

> And when Jesus was baptized, immediately he went up from the water, and behold, the heavens were opened to him, and he saw the Spirit of God descending like a dove and coming to *rest on him*; and behold, a voice from heaven said, "This is my beloved Son, with whom I am well pleased."
>
> Matthew 3:16–17 (italics added)

Noah's name means *rest*.

The Holy Spirit descended like a dove to *rest* on Jesus.

Rest isn't necessarily a place where we do nothing. One of the definitions of rest from dictionary.com is this: "Be placed or supported so as to stay in a specified position. Ex: 'Her elbow was resting on the arm of the sofa.'"

Faith and strength come from a spirit of rest, which is being still long enough to see God move. It's a place of obedience that releases our need to be in charge of the plan, but to keep doing our part.

If Noah teaches us anything right here and right now, it's to never stop sending a resting faith out the window, especially when we are in between the problem and the promise. Even if you are not a naturally patient person (hand raised), there is something very holy for us to hold on to for each of our processes.

> Faith and strength come from a spirit of rest, which is being still long enough to see God move.

Another week passes, Noah gets back up to the window. This time he releases the dove and . . .

Then he waited another seven days and sent forth the dove, and she did not return to him anymore.

Genesis 8:12

Did you catch that? *She did not return.* The dove not returning was the signal they had all been waiting for. The old had gone and a new season was about to begin.

What will we do between the problem and the promise? What will we keep sending out the window? And how will we get from here to there? I think we need to challenge ourselves. . . .

The Gap

Have you ever heard of a high school student graduating and then taking a "gap year"? It's typically defined as a year after high school prior to entering college. This year is designed to give students a little extra time to work on personal growth before entering their next season. There are many public gap-year programs that students can sign up for (and parents can pay for), but a lot of students handle their gap years on their own. They do volunteer work, or they may take some classes on personal growth or even do an internship. Sometimes people who take gap years are seen in a negative light by peers who head straight into college. But goodness, I think it's a brilliant idea.

The place in between the problem and the promise is a gap. From *here* to *there* holds a pause. How long the pause is for each of us varies. But there is a rhythm each of us can embrace despite the various differences in our process. I created this little challenge for myself, and when I feel the need to start trying to take control of things, this has helped me so much. It's based on the acronym G-A-P. Maybe it will help you too.

Remember, this is more about the posture of our hearts, not us doing more.

When I need to raise up my faith in the midst of a problem that is trying to challenge my faith, here's what I've learned to do:

G—Get Settled in the Faith Place
A—Affirm His Plans Again and Again
P—Pray with Passion and Purpose

G—Get Settled in the Faith Place

Sometimes we just have to buckle down and decide where we're going to settle. We can either settle in doubt or we can settle in faith. The choice is ours. Settling in the faith place means we do everything we can to surround ourselves with faith. When we are in between the problem and the promise, we have to have faith speaking to us. Perhaps with Noah, that meant settling close to the window. He would stay close to the place where he knew one day the answer would come.

Tell your friends you need help with faith. Tell your pastor you need help with faith. Tell your soul again and again you need faith. And stay put in the faith place. Don't leave; your promise is coming.

Look to the LORD and his strength; seek his face always.

1 Chronicles 16:11 NIV

A—Affirm His Plans Again and Again

I wonder how many times Noah had to remind himself of the words God spoke to him about His plan. As the Holy Spirit reveals your assignment of belief, remind yourself where you were, what you felt, what you heard. One thing I do almost

151

every single day in my journal is to list ten things I'm believing God for in my life. I have to affirm what God is doing. Not so that He will keep doing His plans, but so that I will remember His plans.

> I will instruct you and teach you in the way you should go; I will counsel you with my eye upon you.
>
> Psalm 32:8

P—Pray with Passion and Purpose

I don't just mean a "help us, Jesus" prayer. I mean a prayer that shakes the ground beneath us. Prayer is **not** our last option. It is the BEST thing we can do in the midst of believing God for breakthrough from the problem to the promise. Keep bringing that problem to God and asking Him for His promise. God never gets tired of us showing up in prayer.

> And pray in the Spirit on all occasions with all kinds of prayers and requests. With this in mind, be alert and always keep on praying for all the Lord's people.
>
> Ephesians 6:18 NIV

If you're not sure about where the gaps are in your life right now, use the chart below and list all the places in your life in which you feel stuck spiritually. Try to identify five things, even if it's something like understanding why God allows things like _____.

Things I feel stuck in:

1. _____

2. _____

3. _____

4. _____

5. _____

Take those five things and write them under the column Where I AM. Then think of what the complete opposite of that place would be and write it under Where I WANT TO BE.

Where I AM	Where I WANT TO BE
Ex: Struggling to believe God's plans are good.	Ex: Waking up each day with a holy expectancy.

Now, define what your G-A-P looks like.

I will settle in the faith place by:
(Ex: getting up early to pray, asking friends to speak faith into me, etc.)

I will affirm this plan over my life:
(Even if it doesn't look clear yet, write down what you believe the plan is.)

I will pray with passion and purpose (write your prayer here):

As this chapter closes and we move to the next, I want you to know I am so proud of you for doing the work you've done so far. Nothing ever returns void when we do it for the goodness of God in our lives. I agree in faith with the prayer you've written above. And I say yes and amen to the plans God has for your life.

CHAPTER 12

When God Calls You Forward

You survived the storm. You trusted God's plan. You obeyed. You embraced the space in between the problem and the promise. Now what? *Transition.*

Transition is this place where we know we're leaving one thing in order to step into what's next. Much like an employee transitions from one job to another or a family transitions from one city to another, each of us experiences transition in our life. Spiritually too.

Some people believe life is one big transition, moving from one season to the next, again and again.

Transition can be a place where we can build our confidence, especially when we clearly see it was God who called us from here to there. Transition is a place where some of the details of our new season become a little clearer, but there is still a deep need to trust God's plan, process, and commands.

During times of transition, it is easy to try to control this part of the process. But if we do that, it could cause us to lose all the efforts we've made to not let doubt sink us.

Remember, God is in charge of the plan, but we are in control of our obedience. *In all spaces and places.*

It's time for Noah and his family to transition from the ark back to the earth. While I am sure there was much relief in knowing that the time had finally come to get off that ark, there must have been some fear, anxiety, and heaviness that weighed on them. After all, there was so much unknown ahead. There were a lot of blank pages waiting to be penned by the hand of God.

> Then God said to Noah, "Go out from the ark, you and your wife, and your sons and your sons' wives with you. Bring out with you every living thing that is with you of all flesh—birds and animals and every creeping thing that creeps on the earth—that they may swarm on the earth, and be fruitful and multiply on the earth."
>
> Genesis 8:15–17

The command we see above in Genesis 8:16 feels very much like the command to enter the ark.

As far as we know, for the year or so that Noah was in the ark, he received no further instructions from God. No encouragement. No "Keep it up, Noah!" No nothing. If this was the first time in months Noah had heard from God, can you imagine what that might have felt like?

Noah had to continue to hold on to the last commands, instructions, and call for obedience God had given him until God called them forward.

Faith reminds us that eventually God does call us into what's next. Faith reminds us that transition is a step in our process.

And faith reminds us that there is always something to look forward to in the next season.

> **Faith reminds us that eventually God does call us into what's next.**

When Kris and I were first looking at buying the Fixer Upper Farm, I felt something deep inside me when I was standing out in the field looking at it all in shambles. I knew it was going to take years to restore and rebuild the property. But I sensed there was going to be a deeper rebuilding and restoring of our marriage, our family, and my calling on this farm. Yet I had no vision while I was standing in the field. I just knew a transition was beginning.

Our first year on the farm revealed the many layers of restoration and rebuilding that needed to happen. In fact, it was a lot of crazy that first year. Our septic system constantly flooded our yard. We would fix things only to have them break again. And trying to rebuild a farm without going into debt proved to be a constant financial tension between Kris and me.

Tension abounded in other areas, like, I wanted new flooring, he wanted the pipes to work. Obviously, his desire for the basic functions around our farm trumped my need to decorate. Friends would stop by for an updated tour of our house in progress and they would ask what we had recently done. I would take them into the bathroom and say, "Please, flush the toilet. It works!"

It didn't feel like what I had sensed was going to happen was actually happening because the tension in the transition was high.

But six years later, I can look back and see how much God has done on this farm. We've had weddings, church events, and revivals, and just a few weeks ago we even had a Barn Prom. This farm has brought a common thread between Kris and me, and it's made our marriage stronger. But as I look ahead, I still see how much there is to do.

That's the weird thing about transition. We have to accept the space between *no longer* and *not yet* and what's coming after that.

Sometimes we can clearly see an ending point. Other times, it feels like there is no end to transition. So I do understand the people who view life as one big transition. For Noah, this process was filled with transition. But the biggest transition of them all was about to take place: from the ark to the earth.

Everybody Out

What a day it must have been for Noah, his family, and all the animals as they were given the command to leave the ark. There are several theories about what it could have looked like.

Some say it's possible Noah was able to reopen the door to the ark that God had closed. Others wonder if Noah initially released all of the flying creatures from their cages and they went through the same window the doves and raven were sent through. There's another theory that possibly Noah cut more exits in the ark so the animals could move out quicker.

And this brings me to the question perhaps many of you are wondering if we will address in this book: Has anyone found the ark, and does it give us clues as to these details?

I wish I had a solid answer for you. But the answer is, no one knows for sure if the ark has ever been found. Several archeologists over the past century claimed they found something resembling the ark in Turkey.

The Ark Encounter scholars have said it's most likely not been found. And they are doubtful it will ever be. Not because they are Negative Nellies. They would love to see the ark discovered just as much as anyone. They just realize a wood structure surviving over 4,300 years in an area that had an active volcano eruption in 1840 is very unlikely.

I'm sure Noah was an EXCELLENT ark builder, but wood rots and decays so easily. Think about how many times a deck on someone's house has to be rebuilt. Barns are considered historic sites if they last longer than a hundred years.

It is possible that people could still see the ark a few thousand years ago, but it's very unlikely you and I have that opportunity today. Which is why the Ark Encounter study trip was so important for me in this process.

While we don't know Noah's exiting plan or process, the Scriptures tell us,

> Every beast, every creeping thing, and every bird, everything that moves on the earth, went out by families from the ark.

> Genesis 8:19

Out But Not Alone

I love that the ESV version of the Bible uses the word *families* to describe the animals exiting the ark together. It's a great picture and reminder that when God calls you into the next season, He's got others to go with you. But unlike the ark, with everyone exiting together, there may be new people to meet you in your transition.

We may feel isolated, but we are not alone.

Because I've lost half of my immediate family in the last few years, one of my prayers is that we would have friends that feel like family. And for a long time, it felt like God wasn't hearing me on that prayer. In fact, when I transitioned from my staff to non-staff position at Proverbs 31 Ministries, one reason I felt so sad was because I felt like I was losing my family. My co-workers were a lifeline to me every day. Many of my former co-workers still feel like friends to me. It's just a different season. We're all doing something different. But it doesn't mean they don't care about me and I don't care about them.

For a season, though, I felt painfully lonely.

The season of relationships within a transition is something we need to pay more attention to. Our relationships with others and with God reflect seasons.

Sometimes the season feels like spring—alive, beautiful, and ready to bloom. Other times it feels like summer, with lots of warm, sunny days and adventures. And then sometimes it feels like fall—a little chilly, with things changing, shifting, and going in a new direction. But honestly, sometimes transition times feel like winter. Dead. Broken. Ugly. Covered with a blanket of snow.

I have a friend who I have seen this so clearly lived out with. We've been friends for almost a decade. There are weeks when we text all the time, hang out, and I feel like I'm super involved with her life and she with mine. But then weeks, even months, will go by and both of us realize, oh gosh, we haven't talked in a long time. Sometimes one of us will wonder if everything is okay. Typically, after a quick phone call, we're good again and we just recognize the season we're in.

If I'm going to be transparent, right now, with all this uncertainty in our world, I feel a little like I'm in a season of fall with God. It's a little chilly. I know things are changing, shifting, and going in a new direction. And I really don't like it.

Now, more than ever, it's time to be intentional about building relationships around us. It might be time to let some relationships with friends or even family fall into a season of winter. But maybe God is about to surprise you in a season that feels like summer, full of adventure and brighter days.

The decision to believe God is in charge despite all these hard situations is one I believe Noah was able to make. But God didn't make Noah do this alone. And God won't make you do this alone. He calls us family.

Ephesians 2:19 says, "So then you are no longer strangers and aliens, but you are fellow citizens with the saints and members of the household of God."

Paul, the author of this verse, is reminding the Gentiles of this promise: They are not alone; they are part of God's family. And this promise holds true today and for every day that will come for you and me.

There are steps you will have to take by yourself. There are decisions you will choose to make alone. But God has people waiting to meet you on the other side of this. It might surprise you who they are and how you will discover them in this transition. You have a family.

Noah and the animals were exiting the ark in families. A whole new world awaited them. It was time to start over . . . or was it?

Starting Over

If you've ever helped someone move, you know it's quite a process to get everything from one house to the next. It can feel overwhelming to even know where to begin when all the boxes begin stacking up in a new house. Kris and I have moved eight times in our nineteen years of marriage, for a variety of reasons. We've stayed put at the Fixer Upper Farm the longest of any place. So in the first fifteen years of our marriage, we averaged a move almost every two years.

Each move was exhausting, especially when the girls were small and couldn't help very much. We had family and friends who would help us move, and we knew the two immediate goals for each new place: 1) get everyone's beds set up, and 2) get the kitchen stuff unpacked. We learned that everything else could wait.

I imagine Noah's wife and their sons' wives had a similar feeling as they stepped off the ark. Shelter and a place to make meals must have been top priorities. The reality is, they probably lived on the ark for some time until new houses could be built.

Unlike the animals who spread out over the earth, Noah, his wife, and their children stayed close together for years to come. While everyone else had a variety of tasks, plans, and dreams for these first moments off the ark, Noah had one priority.

> Then Noah built an altar to the LORD and took some of every clean animal and some of every clean bird and offered burnt offerings on the altar.
>
> Genesis 8:20

Noah put God first. I'm sure he wanted to explore, dream, and plan, but the priority was worship. There was a deep gratitude and grace in Noah for the reality of what this new season meant. It was hopeful and it was hard. The flood washed away the wickedness in the world, but it didn't remove sin from the world. Noah knew that.

I think this is why I struggle when I say or hear things like, "It's time to start over." I love a fresh new page of life as much as anyone, but the reality is in new seasons, our struggles against ourselves still go with us. We get stronger and more faithful the further we go. But new seasons don't always mean new starts.

If we don't deal with the doubt or unbelief in the season we're in, it comes with us into the next.

If we don't deal with doubt and unbelief in the season we're in, it comes with us into the next.

God offers each of us a clean slate. The Bible reminds us that the only thing God forgets is our sin once we seek forgiveness (Jeremiah 31:34). What this means is God isn't holding us hostage for our past. He doesn't dangle our past mistakes in front of us and say, "Remember . . . you did this . . ."

But God's forgiveness cannot be confused with our constant need to put God first. God forgives, God forgets. Unbelief and doubt do not. Which is why it's vital for us to remember God is in charge and God is a priority in our lives. The closer we get to Him each day, the further away our struggle with doubt and unbelief goes.

Had Noah stepped off the ark, begun to build his house, settled his family, and started figuring everything out, it would have been easy to slip into I'm-in-charge mode. Instead, he put himself in the humblest position he could before God. He moved his heart into an immediate place of sacrifice and worship through the building of the altar.

He reminded himself, *God's in charge of the plan, I'm in control of the steps I take toward His plan.*

Noah's process teaches us the need to pause before moving on to what's next. To realign our hearts with God's. And to be fully present before God as one season ends and another begins.

I get why in new seasons we don't take the time to do what Noah did. There are a lot of things to figure out, stuff to do, people to meet, and places to go. But if we're going to take the sober reality of our human nature from one season to the next, there's nothing better to do than to begin like this.

Everything else can wait.

How do we put God first in transition instead of trying to grab control? I'm glad you asked.

I mean, the preacher in me wants to say study your Bible, go to church, surround yourself with the right people, and pray. I want to remind you of verses like Psalm 22:3, which remind us we are created to be worshipers. And that God dwells in our praise. Someone is thinking, *But I can't sing.* It's not about the sound, it's about the sacrifice.

But the friend in me wants to sit beside you and remind you, you won't always get this right. You will reach for control again and again. Also, as a friend, I would want to tell you the best way to release the need to be in control of the situation is to stop looking for a plan and start looking for a promise.

We're about to go into the best part of this message. It's time to start looking for the familiar faithfulness of God and find those promises.

To Find the Familiar Faithfulness of God

CHAPTER 13

God's Familiar Faithfulness

After my mom passed away, my dad decided to move to the coast of South Carolina. I've had a mixed reaction about it. He's too far to just "stop by" but far enough away for a long weekend visit in an ideal location. The latter part I enjoy, but I do worry that if he needed something quickly, it would be hard to get to him. We've been able to visit him several times, and so far, he's made a few friends that can help him in a pinch. Still, I worry.

There's a man who hangs out on the beach near my dad's house. I don't know his name, but our family calls him the *Flat Earth Guy*.

He has a YouTube channel and an entire set-up on the beach, where each day he arrives to try to convince someone the earth is indeed flat. He really believes this and has all kinds of "proof."

One of my daughters decided to sit through one of his presentations. The entire time she was listening to him, Kris and I were looking at each other like, *Is she about to come over here and try to convince us the earth is flat?* We wondered how many hours we were going to have to spend discussing this concept with her. Thankfully, her science classes had taught her well enough for her to settle on the opinion that she didn't believe a flat earth could be true.

The ironic thing was, that very day, I had started following an astronaut on Instagram. He was on a mission for several months in space and was able to Instagram the entire thing. I mean, what a cool world we live in that you can Instagram from space! A very cool, *round* world.

One of the pictures he had just posted was a view from space, and you could see the sphere of the earth. The picture confirmed the roundness of the earth. Yet here was this guy, in real time, trying to convince everyone on the beach that day that the world is flat.

One perspective from above and one from below.

As we continue to step forward into this new place God has met us in throughout this book, there is going to be a need to have a perspective from above. I've been reminded of this as I've continued to watch the news as America has transitioned from a global pandemic crisis to a national race crisis.

Each day it's becoming harder and harder to see things from the perspective of heaven. The perspective from below feels harsh, hopeless, and strange.

The last few months I've been craving anything that feels normal, as I think most of the world is. We want peace. We want justice. We want healing. We want reconciliation. And we want to feel safe. There's a phrase that keeps getting tossed around in the news: "the new normal."

Yesterday I was talking to a friend whose husband is a pastor at a large church in our area. She was explaining to me some of the drastic changes their church has made because of the hard season America has been in for the last year. I was surprised by some of the changes. But at one point she said something that stung my emotions: "We are just very aware church will never be the same."

Even though deep inside me I know that hard seasons bring changes to our lives and society that will forever have a ripple effect, I didn't want to hear this. Perhaps I'm still holding on for church to return to "normal." For school to be in session as "normal," and for my ministry travel to pick back up to "normal."

I keep trying to do things each day like get dressed, put some makeup on, talk to friends, and even dream a little. All in an effort to make life feel "normal." None of it has worked. Because as soon as I leave the front porch of the Fixer Upper Farm, I enter into a city that is anything but normal.

I know there are seasons when your world has been redefined in a new way as well. Some of you are thriving and some of you are barely surviving.

As I've prayed and sought God's wisdom about this new season we're all embarking on, I'm reminded of something: There is nothing normal about our God. The way He created the world, *not normal*. The way He sent Jesus, *not normal*. The way Jesus had to die on a cross, *not normal*. And the way the Holy Spirit works in our lives today, *not normal*.

But the one thing we can see from Noah until today is the familiar faithfulness of God. From one generation to the next, one hard season to another, it is there. The familiar faithfulness of God never leaves us, but we tend to forget about it when faithfulness doesn't feel normal.

So I've been trying to stop looking for normal. And I've been trying to look for His familiar faithfulness in this new season. Even though what I see today may not feel like faithfulness, I know a few thousand feet up in the air, there's an entirely different perspective. I don't want to get wrong what this season means to God because of what I see in front of me.

> Every season still holds God's familiar faithfulness.

This is a new season for all of us. And it won't be the last time life shifts, changes, and becomes something different. But every season still holds God's familiar faithfulness.

We have to look for it, long for it, seek it, and find it . . . with all our heart.

> You will seek me and find me, when you seek me with all your heart.
>
> Jeremiah 29:13

Finding God's familiar faithfulness may come in the presence of our private worship, a Bible verse, a prayer in our journals, a conversation with a friend who loves God, or just a simple walk in nature. His familiar faithfulness is there.

And when I can't see His familiar faithfulness in my life, I can look back on Noah's life and see God's faithfulness. There's something from the past to hold on to for today.

As Noah built an altar to the Lord and began to worship Him (Genesis 8:20), there was something familiar about it. As far as we know, God didn't tell him to build the altar, he just knew to do it. When something feels familiar to us, we just know how to step into it.

There's something from the past to hold on to for today.

It was the same God with Noah before the flood and the same God after the flood. Noah walked with God then, he would walk with Him now. He listened to God then, He would listen to Him now. He would rise above the doubt he had then, and he would rise above the doubt he had now. He would remember God was in charge then and God was in charge now.

The familiar faithfulness of God went into the ark and out of the ark. As we step into this last section of the book, the fifth decision Noah would have to make when life was hard and doubt was rising would be to find the familiar faithfulness of God.

Decision Five: To Find the Familiar Faithfulness of God

As Noah's sacrifice went from earth to heaven, the Bible tells us God was pleased and made a promise:

> And when the LORD smelled the pleasing aroma, the LORD said in his heart, "I will never again curse the ground because of man, for the intention of man's heart is evil from his youth. Neither will I ever again strike down every living creature as I have done. While the earth remains, seedtime and harvest, cold and heat, summer and winter, day and night, shall not cease."
>
> Genesis 8:21–22

In these two verses, God gives two promises: 1) The ground will no longer be cursed by a flood, and 2) there will never again be a universal flood to destroy everything.

But let's stop at that first promise for a minute. The second half of that promise we've seen before: *"For the intention of a man's heart is evil from his youth."*

At the beginning of this book, we saw these same words in Genesis 6:5.

God's heart is the same before and after the flood. Man's heart is the same before and after the flood. Nothing has changed.

But the earth drastically changed. The flood had removed all the seasons for an entire year. There was no fall, winter, summer, or spring during this time. Within this promise to never flood the earth again (Genesis 8:21–22), God reminds us that as long as the earth remains, there will always be seasons, morning and evening, and a time to plant and a time to harvest.

I don't want to get too heavy into this topic because it's way above my study scale. But every day, since this defining day with Noah, we have been moving closer to the return of Jesus. What will this day look like? There are other books and other studies to go to for that biblical insight. But we know that one day, this earth, as it has been known since the days of Noah, will change. Jesus will return to this earth for the second time, this time to defeat Satan once and for all.

Until then, I don't know what it will continue to look like. And I'm not going to pretend like I do.

And what is God waiting for? I really couldn't even begin to guess. I know these days we find ourselves in right here feel hard and heavy. Many of us are jokingly posting memes that say things like, "Jesus, we finished. Come pick us up!"

We may think we're finished. Things may look hopeless today. But there is still work to do. And there is still God's familiar faithfulness to be found.

I want to see revival in our nation and in our world. I want to see the church rise to this occasion to remove the doubt, unbelief, and distrust of God. I really believe there is a unique role each of us is living out in these hard days. The work you've done in the pages of this book internally will eventually turn into something God uses externally.

Your faithfulness in reading, studying, praying, and letting this doubt struggle come to the surface now will allow God's familiar faithfulness to be found in your life tomorrow.

Other than the ground no longer being cursed and the promise to never flood the earth again, what other promises can we count on as we continue to move toward the day Jesus comes back? A lot. There is so much in Scripture we can hold on to. It is estimated there are over 30,000 promises in the Bible. But are they all for us? No. Here's why . . .

Promises and Principles

Maybe this won't be such a shock to some of you, but I've misquoted Scripture before. I'm sure you have too.

Not intentionally. Not because we had a hidden agenda in doing so. And not because we had any earthly idea we were doing such a thing. It is rare to meet someone who could say, "I've never used a verse out of context before." We are all growing, learning, and gaining a better understanding of the Bible.

One place I've seen myself and others do this a lot involves God's promises in the Bible. I've come to understand there's a difference between verses that are considered principles and verses that are promises. Some of these promises are for us and some are promises for someone else in the Bible.

The struggle is, we rarely take the time to figure out which are which. We (including myself) like to take a verse that sounds really encouraging, put it on a cute graphic, and call it a promise from God. Our motives are 100 percent authentic in sharing these promises. We just want people to know and believe how good our God is.

Principles can help us. Promises are guarantees to us.

And He is!

But we need to be cautious to not take promises that were meant for someone else and claim them for ourselves. We also have to be careful we don't take principles and turn them into promises.

Principles can help us. Promises are guarantees to us.

Principles have variables. A promise from God has none.

Principles may not always work. But God cannot lie, so His promises are Yes and Amen.

To better understand this, let's unpack three verses I've mistaken as promises from God. Then I'll show you a few promises I know for sure are for us. Here we go.

1. "Train up a child in the way he should go; even when he is old he will not depart from it."—Proverbs 22:6

I always thought this verse was a promise from God and believed that if I raised my children to love God and know

His Word, they should stay with it, right? Well, in theory, that sounds great, but we all know plenty of people who raised their children under biblical principles, yet those children still turned far from God. This verse is not a promise. This is a principle, because the responsibility falls on the parents, not God.

My girls do love the Lord, but trust me, they have departed from the ways we have raised them more than once. As parents, when we're facing something hard with our kids, we wonder why God's promises aren't being fulfilled in their lives. What we've come to understand through our study of Noah is that God's timing and His ways are beyond our own human comprehension. Principles like this give us hope, something to hold on to. But they aren't a guarantee. Which is hard, because we want guarantees, especially with our doubts.

2. *"I can do all things through him who strengthens me."—Philippians 4:13*

I hesitated to put this verse in here because I know someone just read this and yelled at me, *"WHAT, girl? Yes I can!"*

Writing this right now, I remember that time one of my teenagers had to show me an emoji I was using wrong. It was so awful. But I was thankful she pointed it out to me because it could have been a humiliating situation.

You *can* do a lot of things *because* Christ lives in you. According to the Scriptures, because of Jesus residing within you through His Holy Spirit, you can heal the sick, cleanse the lepers, cast out demons, and even raise the dead (Matthew 10:8). I mean, that's some pretty amazing stuff.

But does that mean you can run a half marathon without training? Dunk a basketball without one practice? Make three million dollars in one day? It's possible! But it's not a promise from God.

This verse in Philippians was written by Paul, who was writing it from prison, where he was being persecuted because of his faith. It was written from a place of showing the endurance he had found in the presence of God for the hardships he was facing because of his faith. This is a verse about learning to be content in all situations.

But that sounds boring, right? It's tempting to use this verse to speak to our doubts. And there are times we need to use this verse to speak into our doubts—especially if someone is questioning our faith—just not when we're trying to make a slam dunk with a basketball for the first time.

3. *"For where two or three are gathered in my name, there I am among them."—Matthew 18:20*

I was a little shocked when I realized this verse is not a promise from God but rather part of the principle of going to someone who has sinned against us and confronting them in love. In Matthew 18:15, Jesus is teaching on how to confront people within the church we might have an issue against. He gives four steps we can take: talk to them in private, take a friend with you to confront them, take it to the church leadership if neither of the former steps work, and, as a last resort and as harsh as this sounds, Scripture says to not have anything to do with them.

Jesus is saying in Matthew 18:20, *I am for resolving things, together. I am for unity. I am for working things out.* But I know I've been tempted to use this verse to confirm the presence of God when we're gathering. The good news is, even when there's just one person, God is there. It doesn't require us having two people.

Okay, let's move on to the better part of this concept: promises for our lives today. Here are a few.

1. *"If you confess with your mouth that Jesus is Lord and believe in your heart that God raised him from the dead, you will be*

saved. For with the heart one believes and is justified, and with the mouth one confesses and is saved."—Romans 10:9–10

Salvation is promised to us. And remember, this isn't just for one day in eternity. It will be an incredible day when we step into eternity, but this is also a promise for TODAY. Salvation is the gift that unlocks the power of the Holy Spirit in our lives.

Some of God's promises have an "if" in front of them, meaning there's something on our part. Notice this one and the one below.

2. *"If any of you lacks wisdom, let him ask God, who gives generously to all without reproach, and it will be given him."—James 1:5*

What a gift this promise is, that we don't have to figure everything out ourselves. In the middle of doubt, hard things, and trying situations, we can ask God for wisdom. How does He show us that wisdom? It comes in a variety of ways. One way is through His Word. Another way is through His Spirit. I think we sometimes underestimate the power of the Holy Spirit in our lives. The Holy Spirit will guide us, nudge us, send the right person to help us. But the key to this promise? *Asking God*. We can't just assume. We need to ask, faithfully and in belief again and again, until we feel confident we have the wisdom we need.

3. *"So faith comes from hearing, and hearing through the word of Christ."—Romans 10:17*

This promise is so good as we continue to wrestle with our own doubts. Faith to believe God's Word is where we are able to receive the promises God has for us. This isn't about seminary degrees, or how much we know about the Bible. It's simply being willing to believe God's Word. It doesn't mean we won't have questions or wonder what things mean or why God did things the way He did. All those things are normal and expected. But this promise—that if we will listen and believe, our faith will increase—is one to hold tight to.

There is not a principle-and-promise police officer patrolling your home for Etsy decor with promises on cute signs and pillow covers to inspect them for theological accuracy. It's okay if you've confused a promise and a principle. ME TOO.

I just think sometimes we find ourselves frustrated with God because we have believed Him for a promise based in the Scriptures to be fulfilled that He never gave us. I know I have been.

God is incredibly merciful with our process with Him. Remember that. He doesn't expect us to have all this figured out.

> Sometimes we find ourselves frustrated with God because we have believed Him for a promise He never gave us.

As we accept that "normal" may never feel exactly like normal again and we start looking for the familiar faithfulness of God, we will be the kind of people who are able to withstand the aftermath of the storm. We'll pick things up, start where things were left off, and step fully into the promises God has for our lives. And we will help lead one generation to the next through the familiar faithfulness of our God.

CHAPTER 14

Rainbows and Bad Days

By now you know how much I love the Fixer Upper Farm. It is truly one of the most peaceful places in my life. For sure, it's filled with ups and downs, but the presence of God on this land is undeniable.

I'm not sure it has much to do with us. Most of the awestruck things we can't explain about God rarely have anything to do with us, anyway.

One of the most incredible things that happens on this farm and makes me feel God's presence so much is the rainbows. Most of the rainbows come in the spring and summer, but occasionally we'll get one in the fall or winter.

There is one spot, between the entrance to the driveway and the front of the house, where these breathtaking rainbows always seem to appear. My phone is full to the max with pictures of rainbows in the exact same spot.

And they always seem to come on the days we need to be reminded of God's promises the most.

The day my agent, Meredith, and I came to an agreement with the publisher of this book, a huge double rainbow appeared in "the spot." Another rainbow came on the day we were waiting on some important news about our adoption. And one of my favorite rainbows came one afternoon as we returned home from running errands.

Hope, my middle daughter, stopped in the middle of the gravel road one day to take a picture of a beautiful rainbow. We then pulled down our driveway to discover about a half-dozen newborn pigs . . . to our surprise! A pot of gold? No, but a pot of pigs!

Obviously, I'm a huge fan of where we're about to head into the account of Noah. It's such a good part of this story. Don't rainbows have this way of making you feel like something special is happening? Well, this is a pretty special moment for Noah.

> And God said, "This is the sign of the covenant that I make between me and you and every living creature that is with you, for all future generations: I have set my bow in the cloud, and it shall be a sign of the covenant between me and the earth. When I bring clouds over the earth and the bow is seen in the clouds, I will remember my covenant that is between me and you and every living creature of all flesh. And the waters shall never again become a flood to destroy all flesh. When the bow is in the clouds, I will see it and remember the everlasting covenant between God and every living creature of all flesh that is on the earth." God said to Noah, "This is the sign of the covenant that I have established between me and all flesh that is on the earth."
>
> Genesis 9:12–17

The Making of a Rainbow

Conditions have to be *just right* for a rainbow to appear. Because we get them so often out here on the Fixer Upper Farm, I've learned how to watch the clouds, the rain, and the sunlight to know when to suspect we're about to get a rainbow. I get so excited too. I'll start telling everyone in my family, "It's about ripe for a rainbow!"

They don't share my enthusiasm, so typically it's just me standing out in the rain waiting for my rainbow.

But if you were out here with me on the farm when the last rainbow appeared a few weeks ago, we would have both stood there and stared as if it was the most wondrous sight ever. We would wonder if God was saying something special to us.

I imagine Noah had similar emotions as he stood there looking at his rainbow.

The rainbow God gave Noah was a long time coming, and now the conditions were just right. While it represented a promise to never destroy the earth by a flood again, it likely represented much more to Noah. It was a reminder of God's mercy. We do not have to fear a worldwide flood again and we do not have to fear a life without God. Because beyond the rainbow, we have Jesus.

> Living intentionally isn't about striving, but it is doing more than just surviving.

We're all about to be in heaven in such a short time. The older I get, the more I realize how deeply true this is. It doesn't mean we just throw caution to the wind and live life however we want to. In fact, it should be the complete opposite. Our days, weeks, and years need to be filled with so much intention.

God's faithfulness helps us remember that living intentionally means we don't have to strive, but in Him, like Noah, we will more than just survive.

What's to come after this? It's for sure going to be amazing. But when I'm ready to take my last breath, I want to exhale knowing I have run as hard as I could after my God. I want to be someone who is willing to take risks, like Noah, to obey God.

Hold tight. Your rainbow is coming.

There is hopelessness in this world. There always has been and always will be. But most hope-filled stories of life come from people who kept going when there seemed to be no hope. Noah is a reminder of that.

Rainbows are a truly majestic part of creation. I don't believe they are ever by accident or a coincidence. They represent the gift after the storm. The next time you see a rainbow, think of Noah but remember your God. May rainbows always feel like the familiar faithfulness of God from Noah until now.

If you haven't seen a rainbow in a while and God's familiar faithfulness feels a little far off for you today, it's okay. Hold tight. Your rainbow is coming.

Dolly Parton said it best: "If you want the rainbow, you gotta put up with the rain."

Even Heroes Have Bad Days

All right, Noah. You built the ark. You wrangled all those animals on and off the ark. You survived the biggest flood anyone on this earth would ever encounter. You worshiped God. You saw your rainbow. You are a hero of our faith. And now you are about to remind us that even heroes have bad days.

Everyone is off the ark. Life is beginning to be lived again, and Noah begins planting a vineyard.

I don't know a lot about gardening. If you read my first book, *5 Habits of a Woman Who Doesn't Quit*, you might remember the story of me accidentally setting my garden on fire. My first-generation farmer roots make an appearance now and then. *Update: Still haven't tried gardening since then.*

But from what I do know, planting anything is tricky. And it takes time.

Many people read this next part of Noah's story and think it happened right after he got off the ark. But let's unpack this a little.

> The sons of Noah who went forth from the ark were Shem, Ham, and Japheth. (Ham was the father of Canaan.) These three were the sons of Noah, and from these the people of the whole earth were dispersed. Noah began to be a man of the soil, and he planted a vineyard.
>
> Genesis 9:18–20

From what I've read through a variety of farming blogs and websites, planting a vineyard takes a lot of time. Most sources said it can take anywhere from two to four years before grapes can start to develop. This I can verify because the Fixer Upper Farm has a few fruit trees, and it took almost four years before any fruit showed up. And to be honest, the fruit that has shown up this summer, our fifth year of having them, isn't really edible. Hopefully next year it will be better.

Let's think this through.

I'm sure it took Noah some time to get settled off the ark. But at the bare minimum, it would have taken him two years to get his vineyard into shape to produce anything. It's possible he had some vines on the ark with him, so maybe it went a little faster than that. Or perhaps he started the vineyard from seeds and it took even longer than that. Regardless, this next scene didn't happen right after the exiting of the ark.

> He drank of the wine and became drunk and lay uncovered in his tent.
>
> Genesis 9:21

Okay. This is a very different side of Noah.

I don't drink alcohol for one main reason. There is a long line of addiction in my family, and when I started to feel this nudge to teach and write, I felt like I needed to leave alcohol alone because it could become a stumbling block for me.

Because have y'all seen my food-related muffin top? I have trouble acknowledging when enough is enough.

But how did Noah, this very put-together, God-fearing, crazy-obedient man, find himself in this, how shall we say . . . *slightly embarrassing* situation?

Well, there are a variety of opinions about this. I'm sure you are as curious as I was about the Ark Encounter's staff opinion on this. Yes, I asked!

A few of them said that it's possible the soil in which Noah planted the vineyard had changed dramatically since the flood—that the wine Noah pressed for the first time post-ark was stronger than the wine he had pre-ark because the soil had changed. There are many other opinions for whether Noah was responsible for this moment or if it truly was a mishap.

Personally, I wondered if one reason he became drunk was from the grief he had experienced or the absolute loneliness he found himself in post-flood. I mean, I have said a few times over the last few stressful months, "I don't drink, but today might be a good day to start."

There's really no biblical backing of any of these opinions. So, in short, we don't know.

We do know this, however: It was a bad day for Noah.

I appreciate moments in stories that humanize people and don't just make them perfect heroes. This is a very human moment for Noah. Still, I hope you can also see the familiar faithfulness of God in these next few verses of Genesis we need to unpack.

Blessing and Curses in the Same Breath

Until now, we have not seen any words spoken from Noah in the entire text we have covered throughout this book. Noah is drunk and finds himself in a tent, naked. His son Ham has done *something* to dishonor him. And finally, the time has come to listen to the words of Noah. Let's pick back up in verse 23:

> Then Shem and Japheth took a garment, laid it on both their shoulders, and walked backward and covered the nakedness of their father. Their faces were turned backward, and they did not see their father's nakedness. When Noah awoke from his wine and knew what his youngest son had done to him, he said, "Cursed be Canaan; a servant of servants shall he be to his brothers."
>
> Genesis 9:23–25

Notice that Shem and Japheth tried to do the honoring thing and cover up their father. This is a clue that maybe Ham didn't share his brothers' same motives toward Noah. It is possible Ham came out of the tent mocking Noah, and these two boys marched straight in there to make it right. Regardless of what happened, Noah found out. And he was m-a-d.

The first words we have in this text from Noah? A curse over Canaan.

Who is Canaan? If you go back to verse 18, we see Canaan is Ham's son.

But why would Noah do this to his grandson if Ham was the one who dishonored him?

Even in my most frustrated moments with my daughters, while I may say something I later need to apologize for, I don't know that I could ever speak a curse over them. No matter how mad I am. It seems strange to me to see Noah, this incredibly godly man who had experienced so much faithfulness from God, speak such harsh words in this moment.

But in the Bible, sometimes a curse is defined as prophetic foresight. Some Bible scholars believe that is what is happening here in Genesis 9:25. Noah is speaking what he sees as insight from God for the future for Canaan.

We see later in the Scriptures these words become true. Canaan settled in an area that would later be known as Israel. The people there would become known as Canaanites. This is significant because later we see a man named Joshua step into an assignment to take out the Canaanites. He also was to take possession of their land and rescue the Hebrews who had been taken captive as slaves.

Perhaps Noah had received this prophecy from God, and he was hesitant to share. But when we're not in our right state of mind, sometimes we say things we wish we would have saved for a better time. Maybe that's what's happening here, maybe not.

The next verse reveals the blessing that Noah speaks over his other sons:

> He also said, "Blessed be the LORD, the God of Shem; and let Canaan be his servant. May God enlarge Japheth, and let him dwell in the tents of Shem, and let Canaan be his servant."
>
> Genesis 9:26–27

During this time, no matter how many daughters were in a family, it was always the son, specifically the first-born son, who received two things from his father: 1) a double portion of the father's wealth, and 2) to become the man in charge of the family. Here we see Noah is dividing this blessing up between Shem and Japheth but is doing nothing for Ham.

I sense there was a deeper divide between Ham and Noah than just this moment of humiliation in the tent. Maybe all that time on the ark had created an unhealthy tension between the two of them.

Despite the curses Noah spoke, Noah is also speaking God's familiar faithfulness through blessing from one generation to the next. And that, I believe, is something for us to pay closer attention to.

Speak Blessing

Have you ever wondered why people say, "God bless you!" after you sneeze? According to the Library of Congress, one of the roots of this phrase can be traced back to Rome when the bubonic plague was running rampant. After someone sneezed, people often said "God bless you!" in the form of a prayer for protection from the plague.

But why do we still use this phrase today? Is it just something that has stuck around after all these years? Or is there more to it?

This is the one place in this book where I will say, don't do what Noah did. Noah is speaking both curse and blessing. But we are not to speak curses over people today. Romans 12:14 gives a clear instruction about this:

Bless those who persecute you; bless and do not curse them.

I love speaking words of hope and positivity, and calling out gifts in people. I am all for saying daily affirmations that align with the Word of God. But I confess, I have missed the need to speak blessings over people.

One of the most famous blessings in the Bible is found in Numbers 6:22–27. Recently, one of my favorite worship leaders, Kari Jobe, wrote a song titled "The Blessing," based on this passage. I think I've played that song at least a hundred times in the last few weeks. It will forever be an anthem for our family.

Blessings are spoken all throughout Scripture. Since it's in there, why do we not do this more—other than after the occasional sneeze?

Speaking a blessing is the act of declaring favor and goodness over people. It's reminding someone who their God is to stir faith in them. And could there be a better way to keep declaring the familiar faithfulness of God than to speak blessing over everyone in our lives?

> Speaking a blessing is reminding someone who their God is.

If faith is stirred through speaking blessings, and faith can change the world, why couldn't we change a few cities, communities, and homes together by deciding to speak blessing over someone each day?

This may feel awkward. It may feel unusual for a while. But what if speaking blessing became as normal to us as sending a text reminder to our kids to have a good day at school, or telling someone we loved them?

Like the principles and promises we find in Scripture, there are also blessings we find.

I want to be a woman who speaks blessings, but I want them to be rooted in the power that is found in the Word, not my words. As we close this chapter, here are five verses you can use as a base to bless someone. I challenge you to bless one person with one of these today.

5 Verses Based on Blessing

Bless someone with the abundance of God:

And God is able to bless you abundantly, so that in all things at all times, having all that you need, you will abound in every good work. As it is written: "They have freely scattered their gifts to the poor; their righteousness endures forever." Now he who supplies seed to the sower and bread for food will also supply and increase your store of seed and will enlarge the harvest of your righteousness. (2 Corinthians 9:8–10 NIV)

Bless someone with the wellness found in God:

Dear friend, I pray that you may enjoy good health and that all may go well with you, even as your soul is getting along well. It gave me great joy when some believers came and testified about your faithfulness to the truth, telling how you continue to walk in it. I have no greater joy than to hear that my children are walking in the truth. (3 John 1:2–4 NIV)

Bless someone with the peace of God:

And the peace of God, which transcends all understanding, will guard your hearts and your minds in Christ Jesus. (Philippians 4:7 NIV)

Bless someone with the hope of what God can do in their life:

Now to him who is able to do immeasurably more than all we ask or imagine, according to his power that is at work within us, to him be glory in the church and in Christ Jesus throughout all generations, for ever and ever! Amen. (Ephesians 3:20–22 NIV)

Bless someone with the strength of God:

Those who hope in the LORD *will renew their strength. They will soar on wings like eagles; they will run and not grow weary, they will walk and not be faint.* (Isaiah 40:31 NIV)

CHAPTER 15

The God We Want

A few months after our horse Princess died, we were left with an ache inside us that wouldn't leave. We would hardly go down to our little white barn because the horse stall that held Princess each night seemed eerily empty.

The saddle Kennedy used to ride Princess sat collecting pollen and dust from the soon-to-be spring season. I missed the sounds of a horse galloping across the field. And I hated how much time Kennedy was spending inside. Her heart hurt. She didn't want to go ride other horses. She wanted her horse, her faithful but sassy friend . . . *Princess.*

Every few weeks we'd ask Kennedy if she was up for getting another horse, and she always said no. Maybe later. Not now.

I'm not a fan of pushing kids past the point they are at emotionally. Grief is something we can't hurry anyone through. But I sensed Kennedy needed a little nudge in the right direction.

And so I asked our horse trainer to keep her ears open if there was another horse who needed a new home. Turns out there were a few horses in need of homes, but none seemed to be a good fit for Kennedy. They were either too old, too short, too small, or too wild. We started to become discouraged, thinking it was going to be way too costly to find a horse like Princess again.

But one afternoon, our trainer texted me about a horse just down the road that needed a home. She was honest to say she wasn't sure he'd be a good fit because he'd been left in a pasture for months and was severely underweight. The temporary owner said the horse had a quirky personality, and our trainer didn't really know what that meant. So she was cautiously optimistic.

I was away on a work trip but texted Kris and Kennedy the details to meet this horse at the farm the next day. I didn't have any information, a name, or a picture of the horse, but he was free . . . and free fit our budget really well. But we also knew we didn't want to get stuck with a horse that was impossible to ride.

So Kris and a very nervous version of Kennedy made their way to the horse farm that Sunday. Our horse trainer brought her saddle and assured me she'd test out the horse before she'd let Kennedy ride.

I wanted this so much for my girl, for her to regain her love and trust of horses. And to feel that familiar faithfulness of riding again. But I didn't want to push it. I knew at the right time the right horse would come.

The text updates from Kris started to come in:

Not sure about this.

He seems friendly but a little wild.

I felt like I held my breath waiting for each update to come in. But then Kris texted that Kennedy was saddling up.

She put on her familiar riding helmet. She climbed the familiar mounting steps. Felt the familiar leather of a saddle as she pulled her body on top of the horse. Slipped her boots into the familiar stirrups. And pulled back the familiar reins. And that familiar wind between a horse's ears blew on her face again as she gave those familiar commands, *"Walk on. Trot."*

Kris filmed the whole thing and sent it to me. Turns out this horse was really amazing. He just needed some love, attention, and a lot of food to put some weight on.

In the midst of all the exciting text updates, I realized I hadn't even asked what his name was. And when Kris texted back his name, tears welled up in my eyes.

Storey.

His name was so fitting for the long season we had found ourselves in of the unknown, loss, and grief. Storey became part of a bigger story in our lives. The one God is writing of familiar faithfulness again and again.

There is a story being written in the midst of your unknown, loss, and grief. Your hard days actually mean something. And you will come out on the other side of every hard, impossible thing different. But you get to decide who you will be. You get to decide how you see your God. How you live out your faith. How you will rise above all the things.

The other day, Kennedy and I were out in the field with Storey. "This horse is way better than Princess," she told me. "I mean, I loved her, but she didn't listen, she was moody, and I could hardly do anything with her. Storey is so sweet, kind, he listens, and he does so many more cool things." And then she said, "Watch this." She proceeded to climb on her saddle and stood up ON THE SADDLE with her arms stretched out wide. "Look, Mom, no hands!"

> Your hard days actually mean something.

I gasped and commanded Storey to not move. Then I laughed. If mothering that child could be summed up in one picture, it was that one.

Just like my Kennedy, I'm not going to push you. Your grief, your loss, your hard days . . . they are yours to wrestle through. But I am going to nudge you just a little. Have you stopped looking ahead because you're still holding on to what was?

Are you needing to release something old for something new? Is there something better just ahead but you can't get there because you're longing for what is gone?

If so, I understand. But perhaps it's time to believe again. And not just belief for the God you want, but for the God He is. His familiar faithfulness will meet you again.

We're All Building Something

> After the flood Noah lived 350 years. All the days of Noah were 950 years, and he died.
>
> Genesis 9:28–29

There's not a whole lot more the Scriptures offer us about Noah's life. These last two verses of Genesis 9:28–29 pretty much sum it up. But this isn't the last time we see Noah's name mentioned in the Bible. It's woven in there throughout a variety of places. His legacy lives on and so does his family.

In chapter 10 of Genesis we see a new genealogy begin. Noah's descendants took the command to be fruitful and multiply (Genesis 9:7) and did that well. But they did not spread out across the earth as the second part of that command said to do. They all pretty much stayed together in a place called Shinar.

Not only did they live there, but they started to build something . . . for themselves: a city and a tower, the Tower of Babel. This didn't please God, so He had to step in, again. This time He gave groups of them different languages and sent them out, with his original command to spread out over the earth (Genesis 11:7–9).

Noah built the ark from faith in God.

Noah's descendants built a tower out of fear.

They wanted to do what they wanted to do. They wanted their God to be the God they wanted Him to be. And since then? Well, I don't have to tell you this again, BUT . . . nothing has changed.

Some of us are building something in faith. And some of us are building something out of fear.

Noah's process has been one of these places where I have wrestled with "God, was there not a better way?" And just because I question the way, it doesn't make God angry.

We want our God to be the same God who was faithful to Noah. But do we want our God to be the same God who looked at humanity and grieved over the condition of their hearts?

We want our God to be the same God who has the power to use wind to part seas and end floods. But do we want our God to be the same God who knew there would never be any power other than Jesus to cure our sin struggle?

We want our God to be the same God who spoke clearly to Noah. But do we want our God to be the same God who called Noah out of a generation to be set apart, different, against the flow of the culture?

I think we would all agree we are living in times when we've never wondered more what God is doing on the earth. Everything feels divided. Opinions have become louder than Truth.

Faith and fear both fight for you to believe in something you cannot see. Choose your battles wisely. Build your life even wiser. Make decisions that lead to obedience.

> Faith and fear both fight for you to believe in something you cannot see. Choose your battles wisely.

As I look back on the last two years of life and reflect on the grief and the loss, I can see God's familiar faithfulness again and again. But I know it's come from a posture in my heart of wanting to walk with God again. Choosing to listen to Him. Rising above all the doubt in my soul. And reminding myself He is in charge.

Noah has taught all of us an important lesson on life, loss, and obedience: We don't get to make the plans, but we get to decide what our process looks like. The steps you've taken throughout this book are your process. And it will be up to you to keep going.

Until we will meet again, on pages filled with words, I bless you with a holy hope that comes from the presence of Jesus. I bless you with faith like Noah that will take you from here to there. And I bless you with the familiar faithfulness of God wherever you go.

You are stronger than you realize. You are wiser than you believe. And you are able to make decisions today that determine the legacy your life story will tell tomorrow.

Never forget, the familiar faithfulness of God follows you wherever you go.

Until we meet again . . . keep making these five decisions when life is hard and doubt is rising.

Decide to . . .

1. **Walk with God**
2. **Listen to God**
3. **Rise above the doubt**
4. **Remember Who is in charge**
5. **Find the familiar faithfulness of God**

> *So proud of you,*
> *Nicki*

Notes

Chapter 1 The Mess of You

1. Sophia Sola, "How Do Mustard Seeds Grow?" Hunker, https://www
.hunker.com/13426703/how-do-mustard-seeds-grow.

Chapter 3 Walk the Line, Barefoot

1. "When Americans Say They Believe in God, What Do They Mean?"
Pew Research Center, April 25, 2018, https://www.pewforum.org/2018/04/25
/when-americans-say-they-believe-in-god-what-do-they-mean/.

2. "Religious Landscape Survey," Pew Research Center, 2014, https://www.
pewforum.org/religious-landscape-study/generational-cohort/#belief
-in-god-trend.

Chapter 5 A Prayer of Belief

1. Atalanta Beaumont, "10 Reasons Why Silence Really Is Golden," *Psychology Today*, April 21, 2017, https://www.psychologytoday.com/us/blog
/handy-hints-humans/201704/10-reasons-why-silence-really-is-golden.

Chapter 10 What Goes Up Must Come Down

1. Pierre Teilhard de Chardin, "Patient Trust," complete poem reprinted
in *Hearts on Fire*, compiled by Michael Harter (Chicago: Loyola Press, 2005),
102.

Nicki Koziarz is a two-time ECPA bestselling author and speaker with Proverbs 31 Ministries. She speaks nationally at conferences, retreats, and meetings, and she hosts her own podcast. An evangelist at heart, Nicki inspires others to become the best version of who God created them to be. Nicki and her husband and three daughters own a small farm just outside of Charlotte, North Carolina, they affectionately call the Fixer Upper Farm.

More from
Nicki Koziarz

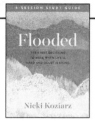

 BETHANY HOUSE

Proverbs 31
MINISTRIES

Know the Truth. Live the Truth.
It changes everything.

If you were inspired by Nicki's book *Flooded* and desire to deepen your own personal relationship with Jesus Christ, Proverbs 31 Ministries has just what you are looking for.

Proverbs 31 Ministries exists to be a trusted friend who will take you by the hand and walk by your side, leading you one step closer to the heart of God through

- Free online daily devotions
- First 5 Bible study app
- Online Bible Studies
- Podcast
- COMPEL Writer Training
- She Speaks Conference
- Books and resources

Our desire is to help you to know the Truth and live the Truth. Because when you do, it changes everything.

For more information about Proverbs 31 Ministries,
visit www.Proverbs31.org.